SUTTON POCKET HISTORIES

THE
INCAS

NICHOLAS J. SAUNDERS

SUTTON PUBLISHING

First published in the United Kingdom in 2000 by
Sutton Publishing Limited · Phoenix Mill
Thrupp · Stroud · Gloucestershire · GL5 2BU

British Library Cataloguing in Publication Data
A catalogue record for this book is available from the British
Library.

ISBN 0-7509-2399-7

*Cover picture: Inca gold figure, AD 1470–1532, Peru. Photo by David
Heald (courtesy of the National Museum of the American Indian,
Smithsonian Institution)*

 ALAN SUTTON™ and SUTTON™ are the
trade marks of Sutton Publishing Limited

Typeset in 11/16 pt Baskerville.
Typesetting and origination by
Sutton Publishing Limited.
Printed in Great Britain by
Bath Press, Bath.

985.019 SAU

For my parents

Contents

List of Maps

List of Dates

INCA:

The early period of Inca history is riddled with ambiguity and confusion. Neither the Incas nor their contemporaries kept written records, nor did they reckon an individual's age by the passage of years, but rather by the kind of work they were able to undertake. They also mixed myth and history, and rewrote royal genealogies as the empire expanded and according to the outcome of internal political intrigues. While Pachacuti Inca was the first true emperor, his predecessors as Inca rulers were probably little more than chiefs in the Cuzco region and they remain shadowy figures. Their dates are impossible to establish though a rough starting date for the Inca dynasty may be around AD 1200. Nevertheless, records were kept as oral history and on knotted strings known as *quipu*, and a variety of sometimes contradictory accounts were given to the Spanish after the conquest in 1532. As a result, the sequence of these early rulers is usually given as follows.

Manco Capac
Sinchi Roca
Lloque Yupanqui
Mayta Capac
Capac Yupanqui
Inca Roca
Yahuar Huacac
Viracocha Inca

1438   Pachacuti Inca defeats the Chanca and becomes emperor.

1463   Pachacuti's son, Tupac Yupanqui, takes command of the army.

1471   Tupac Yupanqui succeeds Pachacuti.

1493   Huayna Capac succeeds Tupac Yupanqui as emperor.

1527   Huayna Capac dies without naming an heir; his son Huascar is recognized as emperor in Cuzco.

1527–32 Civil war between Huascar and Atahualpa.

1532   Atahualpa wins civil war; Spanish arrive.

1533   Huascar executed on Atahualpa's orders; Atahualpa executed by Francisco Pizarro; Tupac Huallpa becomes puppet emperor and is assassinated; Manco Inca replaces Tupac Huallpa.

1536–7   Siege of Cuzco by the Incas.

1541   Francisco Pizarro and Diego de Almagro are killed by each other's supporters.

1545   Manco Inca killed by Spanish at Vitcos.

1571   Inca Titu Cusi Yupanqui dies at Vilcabamba and is succeeded by Tupac Amaru.

1572   Spanish capture Tupac Amaru at Vilcabamba, and execute him in Cuzco.

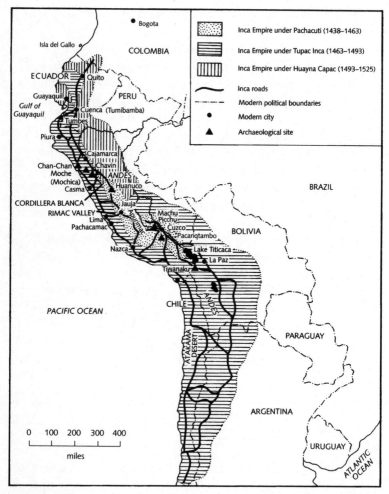

The Inca Empire

Introduction: The Andes, Living Landscapes

In South America, the snow-capped Andean Cordillera was home to some of the world's greatest civilizations. For over three thousand years, in what today are the modern nations of Peru, Bolivia, Ecuador, Argentina, Colombia and Chile, Pre-Columbian peoples flourished in the starkly contrasting landscapes of the region.

The Andes rise to over 7,000 m, pushed up by tectonic forces caused by the Pacific Ocean floor sliding beneath the continental mainland. They stretch from the Caribbean coast of Colombia in the north down to Chile in the south, where they dip beneath the freezing waters of the Southern Ocean at Cape Horn. The Central Andes have three distinct geographical areas. On the eastern slopes begin the tropical rainforests that stretch away to the Atlantic. To the west is a thin strip of coastal desert that borders the Pacific Ocean and is cut by westward flowing rivers from the highlands. In between, the mountains themselves form a high altitude barrier between coast and jungle. The proximity of these three different environments encouraged craft specialization and stimulated trade in materials and ideas between the regions from early on.

The whole Andean region is a land of fire and ice, wracked by earthquakes and volcanic eruptions which can devastate whole areas. In AD 1600 in southern Peru, a violent explosion blew away the whole of a volcano, covered a vast area with volcanic ash, and killed tens of thousands of people. On the coast, earth tremors can also bring tidal waves which sweep away every sign of life. Even worse is the natural disaster known as El Niño. This climatic event causes a shift in ocean currents and weather patterns which brings a burning drought to the southern Andes and torrential rains and flash floods to the north coast.

In such a volatile landscape, humans appeared powerless before the forces of nature. Their response was to regard these natural phenomena as gods in human form, and see the natural world as alive with spiritual power. In this way, the native peoples of the Andes believed they could control or at least placate their dangerous and unpredictable environment through worship and sacrifice. Snow-capped volcanoes, glittering icefields, fast-flowing rivers, and endless deserts became sacred places, embodiments of ancestral forces which played important roles in mythology. Together with the sun, moon and stars, the worldview of South America's indigenous peoples was one where the natural and supernatural mixed together. Animals, plants, human beings, and even the objects they made, were caught up in a shape-shifting universe where good and evil spirits mingled freely and only the power of religion stood between survival and disaster.

The Incas took the ideas of supernatural ancestors, caves, earthquakes and storms, and made them into epic stories or myths. These myths played on ideas of transformation which came from observing the rapid changes and often spectacular dramas of the natural world. Prominent mountain peaks produced local weather conditions and thus were seen as masters of crop and animal fertility. People went on pilgrimages that linked the everyday life of the village with sacred places such as tombs, sites of human and animal sacrifice, and snowfields which were seen as the sources of life-giving water. In this age-old tradition, which continues today, the ancestors were linked to the living, the past to the present, and all life to the sacred earth. For Andean peoples the world was a place of drama and spectacle. The shimmering bodies of supernatural beings were glimpsed everywhere – in the flash of lightning, blinding snowstorms, sunrise, sunset, and the glitter of sacred minerals and metals. The peoples of the Andes saw the physical world as a reflection of the spirit realm – a place where magical encounters took place, and epic struggles between humans and gods were resolved.

This world is as strange and unfamiliar to us as it was to the Spanish conquistadors who first encountered it in the early sixteenth century. The Incas and their neighbours seemed to inhabit a parallel universe of feelings and connections which owed little to European logic or experience. For Amerindians, the retelling of myths could bring objects to life and, by wearing or displaying certain items, memories and stories could be triggered and retold as myths. Pottery made from clay, clothing spun from cotton, and jewellery of shells, gemstones or precious metals were all objects known to the Spanish. Yet their importance for the Incas came not from their commercial value but from the spiritual qualities with which they were endowed.

This clash of indigenous and western worldviews is seen famously in different attitudes towards gold and to the legend of El Dorado, the so-called 'Golden Man'. For the Incas and other indigenous peoples gold had no commercial worth, but was widely considered as bestowing the 'breath of life'. It was a sacred incorruptible substance, associated with the shinyness of crystals, silver and sunlight. When mixed with other metals, especially copper, gold was a symbol of life and fertility. For Europeans such ideas were incomprehensible. They saw gold as the world's most valuable material with which one could buy anything one's heart desired.

When Europeans heard stories of an Amerindian chief covered in gold their imaginations took flight and El Dorado became a great golden city full of unimaginable riches. The truth was different. In the Andes of Colombia, there was a tribe who appointed a new chief by anointing him with resin and gold dust and casting gold into a lake as an offering to the ancestors. The lake's waters once had flowed as rivers, originating as rain which fell from the skies – a physical and spiritual recycling of precious water. Amerindians and Europeans saw very different things even when they looked at the same object.

PRE-INCA CIVILIZATIONS

The first Americans were human settlers who crossed the Bering land-bridge from Siberia to Alaska perhaps as early as 20,000 years ago. They spread out through North, then Central America, and reached southern Chile in South America about 13,000 years ago. These early hunters and gatherers flourished, adapting to the range of environments, from tropical rainforests to rolling grasslands, and from deserts to the high mountains of the Andes. By around 2,000 BC huge cities made of stone blocks and mud brick (adobe) were being built in the lush river valleys which cut across Peru's dry coastal deserts.

The early features of civilized life came together at the famous site of Chavín de Huántar. Between 800 BC and 200 BC, Chavín's inhabitants created a dramatic art style where jaguars, eagles and caymans were shown alongside fanged supernatural creatures on pottery, textiles and goldwork. Chavín de Huántar was a religious centre, and its finely wrought stone architecture was dominated by ceremonial buildings. One of the most impressive structures is a U-shaped platform whose interior passageways lead to a huge carved-stone image of a half-human, half-feline deity. The outer temple walls were once covered with fearsome carved heads decorated with snakes, fangs and staring eyes. The technological innovations, religious beliefs and art-style of the Chavín culture had a powerful influence on many later civilizations, and the site remained a pilgrimage centre into Inca times.

As the Chavín culture declined, the Mochica

culture (200 BC–AD 650) came to prominence on Peru's north coast. The Mochica are famous for their rich and expressive pottery, with which they represented everyday activities as well as mythological and religious scenes. They also constructed monumental architecture. It took 100 million adobes to build just one structure, the famous 'Pyramid of the Sun'. Recent excavations at the site of Sipán have yielded an extraordinary wealth of golden artifacts from the burials of Mochica priest- rulers. Around AD 600, Mochica culture collapsed, probably as a result of an El Niño.

Contemporary with the Mochica were the Nasca people who lived on Peru's south coast between AD 100 and AD 650. Nasca potters were master craftsmen who used many colours to paint their ceramics with a dazzling array of real and imaginary creatures. Human trophy heads feature prominently in their art, indicating warfare and head-hunting. Nasca is most famous for its huge desert drawings. Long lines and gigantic animal images, such as the condor, monkey and killer whale, were etched into the desert's surface. Some possibly had astronomical significance, while others may have been associated with pilgrimages and rain ceremonies.

As the Mochica and Nasca cultures faded on the coast, an important new culture was spreading its influence in the central highlands of Peru. The Wari culture (AD 400–AD 800) added new features to Andean culture by inventing roadbuilding, large-scale planned architecture, agricultural terracing and bronze working. They also introduced the South American equivalent of writing, the knotted strings known as *quipu*. At its height, the city of Wari probably had anywhere between 10,000 and 70,000 inhabitants. Further south, around the southern shores of Lake Titicaca, the great city of Tiwanaku rose to prominence at more or less the same time, around AD 650–700. This huge ceremonial city has many large buildings and temples. One of these had elaborate drains and spouts, which probably made it appear like a vast sacred fountain. In another part of the city is the famous 'Gateway of the Sun', a giant doorway carved from one huge slab of stone. At its peak, Tiwanaku was the hub of an empire whose llama caravans connected vast areas of southern Peru and northern Chile.

The last of the great pre-Inca cultures was that of the Chimú which appeared in the area previously occupied by the Mochica between AD 1000 and AD 1476. The Chimú capital of Chan-Chan sprawled across 20 sq km, and housed around 30,000 people. It was composed of giant compounds which, as with later Inca buildings, served as royal palaces during a ruler's lifetime, and his mausoleum after death. The Chimú were an imperial society and, under their god-like rulers, created a large coastal empire which stretched along Peru's north coast. They fell ultimately to the Inca armies from Cuzco.

This brief overview shows the rise of the Incas was set against the background traditions of many South American civilizations. While the scale of the Inca achievement was unparalleled, the building blocks of their success were the accumulated inventions, achievements and religious traditions of their predecessors, stretching back thousands of years into the Pre-Columbian past.

ONE

Creating the World

For the native peoples of the Andes, mythology was not a collection of superstitious beliefs and fanciful stories. It was a living reality, a way of seeing the world and of understanding and celebrating how things had come to be as they are. Mythology illuminated the mysteries of life and death, and the language used to recount individual myths was vivid and memorable. The favourite topics of myths concerned the origins of human beings, the magical role of ancestors, and the continued well-being and fertility of land, livestock and people. Despite local and regional differences, most myths focused on gods and events which symbolized the realities of living in a violent and unpredictable land.

Across the Andes, creation myths told epic stories of how order was created from chaos, and light from the darkness. Common themes told how founding ancestors had emerged from caves or lakes, how rocks had turned into people and back again, and how the social order was bestowed on humans by the gods. They explained how, in order to maintain the universe, people had to carry out sacrifices and rituals at particular times and places, and go on sacred pilgrimages.

Myths also gave the seal of approval to the high social status of chiefs, priests, kings and emperors, by tracing their beginnings back to a distant past where they had first been given divine status. In short, Andean myths provided a framework for living, and a spiritual origin for ethnic identity. For imperial cultures, mythology could also be used to justify military expansion as well as to enforce the duties of common people to take up arms. As empires expanded their mythologies tended to become more elaborate, as they had to take account of the traditions and beliefs of newly conquered peoples. Nowhere was this more true than with the Incas.

INCA CREATION MYTHS

The Incas drew inspiration from the stories and traditions of their neighbours and predecessors as well as from their mountainous surroundings for their mythology. These different influences can be seen in a cycle of creation myths in which Lake Titicaca played a leading role. So important was Titicaca in Inca mythology that the Incas built commemorative temples on the Island of the Sun in the middle of the lake. As the largest body of water in South America, Lake Titicaca was an important 'place of emergence' for peoples of the southern Andes, a metaphor for spiritual rebirth with strong ties in religious terms to the Pacific Ocean as 'mother of fertility'.

Among those peoples who lived in the area around Lake Titicaca before the Incas there existed many creation stories and culture heroes. One of these supernatural figures, called Thunapa, was regarded as 'the bringer of civilization'. The descriptions and stories surrounding this hero figure later became entangled with those associated with the Inca creator god Viracocha, and probably also were further influenced by Christian missionaries and their stories of the apostles.

According to one version of the myth, Thunapa arrived from the north with five followers. He was a striking and impressive man, with blue eyes and a beard, and he preached against war, drunkenness and the taking of more than one wife. He carried a wooden cross on his back to the city of Carapucu and left his followers there while he visited another village. During his absence, trouble began when one of his followers fell in love with the daughter of a chieftain called Makuri. On his return, Thunapa baptized the girl. Makuri was so angry that he killed the disciples and left Thunapa for dead. The hero's body was placed in a totora reed boat and set adrift on Lake Titicaca whereupon it magically began to move at great speed of its own accord. The boat rammed into the lake shore so hard that it created a river, and on these fast-flowing waters Thunapa's body was borne away westwards to the Pacific Ocean.

While such stories show strong Christian influence, their origins are Pre-Columbian, and probably pre-Inca as well. Another version of world creation is found in the writings of the half-Spanish, half-Inca chronicler, Garcilaso de la Vega. He tells how, in ancient times, the world was full of mountains, and the people who inhabited it lived like wild beasts. They had no religion and no social order. Lacking any sense of morality they slept with each other's wives, and lived without houses or cities. In groups of two or three they inhabited caves and rock crevices, wore no clothing, and did not even know how to make cotton or wool. Rather than cultivate the land, they ate human flesh and wild plants.

The Sun looked on these wild creatures with pity, and sent two of his children, a boy and a girl, to teach them how to lead a civilized life, and how to worship him as their god. The Sun set his children onto the earth near Lake Titicaca with instructions to thrust a rod of solid gold into the soil wherever they stopped to eat or rest. At the place where the rod sank easily into the earth, there they should build the sacred city of the Sun. He then told them to feed, organize and protect the people whom they civilized, and to treat them as their own beloved

5

children in the same way as he had cared for them. 'Imitate my example,' he said. 'I give them my light and brightness . . . I warm them . . . I grow their pastures and crops . . . bring fruit to their trees, . . . and bring rain and calm weather by turns.' The Sun then promised to make his two children the rulers and lords of all whom they instructed and cared for in the manner he had outlined. The Sun then departed, leaving his children to make their way from Lake Titicaca and journey northwards, stopping at many places to test the golden rod.

Eventually they came to a small building known as Pacariqtambo, or the 'Inn of the Dawn'. From here they were able to walk to the Valley of Cuzco which at that time was a wilderness. At a place called Huanacauri, they pushed the golden rod into the earth and it sank immediately until it was out of sight. Satisfied that they had found the place foretold by their father, the pair split up and travelled across the length and breadth of the land and gathered together the varied peoples of the world. These they impressed with their appearance, fine clothing and knowledge of civilized living. As the numbers of followers grew, they began worshipping the heavenly pair as living gods and obeyed them as their kings. In this way, Garcilaso says, the great Inca city of Cuzco was filled with people.

Understanding Inca myths can be difficult and it is often impossible to get a clear picture of the events they record. As a mix of previous and contemporary traditions, Inca myths occur in many different and overlapping versions. A variation of the Inca creation tells how three brothers and three sisters were the ancestors of the Incas, and how they emerged into the world from three caves at Pacariqtambo. One brother, Ayar Cachi, angered the others by performing great feats of strength, hurling his magic slingstones and thereby shaping the Andean landscape. Jealous of this display, his brothers tricked him into returning to Pacariqtambo whereupon they sealed up the cave behind him. Nevertheless, Ayar Cachi escaped, telling his brothers that they should wear golden earrings as a sign of their royal status. At the mountain called Huanacauri, Ayar Cachi reappeared and turned himself and a brother into stone. The remaining brother, Manco Capac, then founded the city of Cuzco on the site later occupied by the Temple of the Sun God, Inti.

A common theme in such myths emphasizes the repeated attempts by the gods to perfect their handiwork by successive creations. In another Inca myth we see how Viracocha first created a world of darkness inhabited by a race of great stone giants. When they ignored his wishes, he punished them by sending a great flood to destroy the world. Everything perished except one man and one woman, who were magically taken to the god's home at Tiwanaku. Viracocha tried a second time, making people out of clay, painting onto them the clothes whose varied designs and colours distinguished one nation (or ethnic group) from another. He also gave each group its own language and customs. Then Viracocha blew his divine breath into them and thereby brought his models to life. He sent them to earth and commanded them to emerge from the natural features of the landscape – caves, lakes and mountains. At each place of emergence they were told to honour their maker by building shrines for his worship.

Pleased with his success, Viracocha then created light from the darkness – order from chaos – so that his people could see and live in a safe and orderly world. He caused the sun, moon and stars to rise up to the heavens from the Island of the Sun in Lake Titicaca. As the sun ascended into the sky at the first dawn, the god cried out to the Inca people and their leader Manco Capac, foretelling that they would be great conquerors and the lords of many nations. As a divine blessing, Viracocha gave Manco Capac a beautiful headdress and a great battle-axe as signs of his royal status among men. Manco then led his brothers and sisters into the heart of the earth, from where they emerged into the daylight once more at the place of three caves known as Pacariqtambo.

The importance of traditional Andean ways of representing the landscape in mythological terms can be appreciated by the way in which the archaeological ruins of previous civilizations feature in these epic stories. The great pre-Inca city of Tiwanaku by the shores of Lake Titicaca was regarded by the Incas as the place where Viracocha first set out a new world order, sending the first man and wife out from the ruined city to call forth Andean peoples from every feature of the landscape.

Despite their many different forms, Inca creation myths share several features in common. They served to establish the royal prerogatives of the Inca ruling dynasty, thereby providing a sacred precedent for the high social status and privileges of Inca royalty. More generally, such stories offered a dramatic account of the supernatural origins of their physical surroundings, and explained how and why mountains, lakes, rivers and shrines were located in particular places and how they became full of supernatural power.

Inca myths made use of age-old ideas, especially the belief in transformation. The ability of culture heroes to change into rocks and stones, or of these inanimate objects to adopt human form, give supernatural help and then revert back to their original shape, is a constant theme in the Andes. This magical quality of stone is one explanation why mountains, rocky outcrops, carved statues and columns, as well as stone-built temples and pyramids, held such significance for the Incas and their predecessors.

At heart, creation myths relate ideas of the spiritual unity of people and landscape, of sacred places, magical journeys, and the appearance of human beings at the dawning of first light. These beliefs were far older than Inca culture, but were woven by the Incas into a grand new imperial design which became ever more elaborate as their empire expanded. Inca mythology was often quite literally set in stone, and reinforced the propaganda that it was the Incas and their gods which had created the world and brought civilization to it.

TWO

Inca Religion

A WORLD OF SPIRITS

In a universe ruled by ancestor spirits and powerful supernatural forces, mythology and religion were never far apart. For thousands of years, Andean peoples had come to terms with their environment and tailored their spiritual life accordingly. The Incas adapted some of these ideas and invented others so that their religion was but a grander imperial version of what had gone before.

Inca religion served the purposes of the Inca state with a ritual calendar of festivals at which the gods, the mummies of past emperors and the reigning monarch were all venerated. Their typically Andean worldview saw land, sky and water not as discrete parts of the world, but as elements of an integrated

12

whole infused with spiritual life and criss-crossed by invisible lines of supernatural power. The origin of this power was enshrined in mythology and appeared in temples, tombs and sacred places. Such ideas were tenacious. They survived the Spanish conquest, absorbed Christian influences, and can be seen today among the contemporary Quechua and Aymara peoples, the modern descendants of the Incas.

A common feature of religious life is the idea of the sacred place – a physical location believed to contain mythical importance and supernatural power. These special places became the focus of religious activity. They are generally referred to as *huacas*, and can be springs, lakes, rocks, caves, mountains, and the tombs of ancestors. Importantly, they can also be long-abandoned temples and cities built by previous cultures. With no writing system to record earlier cultures, the oral accounts saw these architectural remains in mythological terms as the work of ancestral beings.

One of the most common types of *huacas* are *apachetas*, piles of small stones strategically placed along mountain paths, or at crossroads. Here, travellers may place another stone, offer coca leaves, deposit a sea shell or deliberately spill *chicha* (maize beer) as an offering to local spirits before continuing their journey. Such beliefs link the present and the past, and recall the Inca legend which tells how rocks turned briefly into men in order to help the emperor Pachacuti defeat his enemies the Chanca.

The most impressive *huacas* are the sacred mountains whose snowcapped peaks everywhere dominate the Andean skyline. Throughout the Inca empire, local towns and villages had their own important mountains. These were linked, one to another, in a system of sacred peaks which tied the empire together ideologically as well as geographically. Overlooking Cuzco are two prominent mountains, the 'brothers' Salcantay and Ausangate. They are regarded as the 'fathers' of all mountains, and are often invoked in rituals which pray to other smaller mountains for good weather and crop fertility. Salcantay is commonly referred to as Apu or Lord, and local people appeal to its power in order to cure illness and disease. Yet, like all spirit-mountains, Salcantay can turn against humans as well as help them. If displeased it sends biting winds, snowstorms or sleet to damage crops and kill valuable livestock. Those who today pass near take care to make offerings and placate its anger.

Andean beliefs about the supernatural nature of mountains and stones have been called a kind of 'sacred geography'. They had an important impact on the location and style of Inca architecture. The often huge granite blocks which the Incas used to construct their monumental buildings themselves came from quarries located on the flanks of 'living' mountains. Temples, fortresses and palaces were all made from these sacred raw materials, as well as being built in a style which defied the earthshaking tremors that are a feature of the region.

At Machu Picchu, one of South America's most impressive archaeological sites, the combined effect of sacred and physical geography is spectacular. The mountain-top city covers 100 acres, and its finely wrought stone masonry includes temples, palaces, houses, terraced fields, and an elaborate system of water conduits and fountains. Although Machu Picchu may have been a royal estate, its true significance may lie in its relationship with other sacred mountains nearby. At the centre of the city is a carved-stone pillar known as the *intihuatana* or 'hitching post of the sun'. Although commonly regarded as having an astronomical purpose, it may in fact have been associated with mountain worship, located at a point where sacred peaks were in alignment with the cardinal directions.

Mountains reach up to the sky and at the horizon the earth and heavens meet. The power attributed to celestial phenomena is seen in religious beliefs which linked earthly events with those in the night sky. The cluster of stars known as the Pleiades were called *Collca* (the granary) by the Incas, and were considered to be the celestial guardians of seeds and agriculture. Inca priests used the Pleiades to calculate a lunar calendar, and for divination in rituals of agricultural fertility and animal husbandry. In the month of April, for example, a pure white llama was dressed in red and taught to eat coca leaves and drink *chicha*. The Incas believed this symbolized the first llama which appeared on earth after a primordial flood. Another constellation was *Orqo-Cilay* (the

16

multi-coloured llama), and this was believed to protect the royal llama flocks.

Inca astronomer-priests were not astronomers in the modern sense. Their precise observations of sunrise and sunset, and of the phases and movements of the moon were carried out in order to calculate the two most important religious festivals in Cuzco – the December and June solstices. The December solstice saw the celebration of *Capac Raymi* – the 'royal feast' – the main feature of which was the initiation into adulthood of young boys of royal blood. At this important time, the sun was observed at sunset from the *Coricancha* – the main temple of the sun god Inti. This event may have marked the beginning of the new year. Elaborate festivities also took place at the June solstice during *Inti Raymi*, the festival specially dedicated to Inti.

Some of the most important insights into Inca religion and astronomy concern the Milky Way and its unique 'dark cloud' constellations made up of opaque patches of interstellar dust. These include *Yacana*, the llama, and *Yutu-yutu*, the tinamou (a partridge-like bird). According to mythology, when the celestial llama disappears beneath the horizon at midnight it is believed to be drinking water from the earth and thereby preventing flooding. Llamas were among the most prized sacrificial animals for the Incas, and were offered on mountain-tops at the new moon. Black llamas were starved during October in order to make them weep and thereby sympathetically ask the gods for rain.

In 1571 the Spanish chronicler, Polo de Ondegardo, wrote that among the Incas all of the earth's animals and birds had their likenesses in the sky, and that these were responsible for the procreation and well-being of their terrestial counterparts. Even today, throughout the Andes, there are many echoes of these ancient beliefs.

In the modern Quechua village of Misminay, near Cuzco, animal constellations and the Milky Way continue to exert a powerful influence on local mythology and cosmology, as well as on all important cycles of earthly fertility. The Vilcanota (Urubamba) river is regarded as an earthly reflection of the Milky Way as it arches across the night sky. Both the Vilcanota and the Milky Way are seen as rivers, and together are responsible for the recycling of water from earth to sky, whence it eventually falls again to earth as rain. The people of Misminay, like their Inca predecessors, also recognize dark cloud constellations, such as the llama, fox, toad and serpent. They are closely associated with Pacha Mama, the earth mother, in whose subterranean depths all animals originated. The mixing of astronomy, mythology and the natural life cycles of animals is seen when two stars (called 'the eyes of the llama') rise before dawn in late November and December. It is at this time that earthly llamas give birth. Similarly, when the Sun and the constellation of the fox rise together in the south-east around the December solstice, young foxes are born on a nearby mountain. Dark cloud constellations are also related to the rainy season and atmospheric phenomena. The constellation of the serpent, for example, is visible in the sky during the rainy season, but is 'below ground' (i.e. beneath the horizon) during the dry season. For Misminay's inhabitants, this corresponds to the apparent emergence from the ground of rainbows (regarded as multi-coloured serpents) which follow the rains and subsequently disappear as the air dries.

During Inca times, the imperial capital of Cuzco was the focus of religious and political activity. As the 'navel of the world' it was the intersection of sacred space and sacred earth. Such ideas are nowhere more apparent than in the *ceque* system. *Ceques* were imaginary straight 'lines' radiating out from the Coricancha Sun Temple like the spokes of a wheel. These lines of power traversed the city, and reached out beyond the horizon of the Valley of Cuzco to the empire beyond. They divided land and space, and imposed order on the everyday and spiritual lives of the people.

Each line had many *huacas* distributed along it. A total of some 328 *huacas* were dotted along the 41 *ceques* in the immediate area of the city. In 1551 the Spanish chronicler Juan de Betanzos described the sixth *huaca* lying on the sixth *ceque* of Antisuyu as 'the house of the puma', where the mummy of Inca Tupac Yupanqui's wife was preserved and where young children were offered as sacrifices. Other *huacas* placed along these lines were associated more directly with geographical features, such as springs, caves and rocky outcrops. The *ceque* system also had astronomical associations. Prayers, processions and sacrifices were associated with individual *huacas* and particular *ceques*, and were timed in accordance with the calendar. A practical aspect of the system was the allocation of water rights – a longstanding concern in the highlands.

It was this world of spirits and spirit power which defined the Andean landscape for the Incas and their contemporaries. Against this background they created their own distinctive pantheon of gods – powerful supernaturals who took the form of sky deities and who, while inspired by age-old beliefs, were nevertheless distinctively Inca.

THE INCA GODS

Viracocha reigned supreme over all other Inca gods. He was an ever-present creator deity who remained remote from the everyday affairs of men and women. He had set the universe in motion by breathing his magical breath into the humans, animals, plants and lesser gods he had fashioned, and then retired into the cosmic background.

After having created the world, Viracocha travelled throughout his dominions performing miracles, shaping the landscape and instructing his people how to live. Inca mythology records some of these magical journeys, telling how, on reaching the town of Manta in Ecuador, he set out on a raft into the Pacific Ocean. When the Spanish arrived by sea to discover Peru in 1532 they were seen as emissaries of the god, and were referred to as *viracochas* – a term of respect still used today by modern Quechua peoples. When the conquistadors finally arrived in the Inca capital Cuzco, they saw a golden statue of the deity shown in human form as a bearded white man wearing a long tunic.

Although widely regarded as the source of all divine power, the creator differed from all other gods in that he had no name. Viracocha was merely a term of respect. He did however possess a number of titles which befitted his primordial status, among which was *Ilya-Tiqsi Wiraqoca Pacayacaciq* – or 'Ancient foundation, lord, instructor of the world'.

This tongue-twister was shortened by the Spanish to Viracocha.

Viracocha delegated the affairs of everyday life to more active deities – powerful sky gods, who presided over the heavens or dwelt atop snowcapped mountain peaks. They sent rain, hail, lightning, drought and earthquakes to afflict the land and had to be appeased if disaster was to be avoided. For the Incas, these elemental gods embodied the forces of nature, and their worship of them linked the world of people with that of the spirit realm.

Of these active deities, Inti – the Sun god – was the divine ancestor of the Inca royal dynasty. Represented as a golden disk surrounded by sunrays and with a human face, Inti was the focus of elaborate state rituals which took place in his golden temple, the Coricancha in Cuzco. Here, his shimmering solar image was flanked by the elaborately dressed mummies of dead emperors, and surrounded by walls covered in sheets of gold – the sacred 'sweat of the Sun'. The spiritual connections between gold and Inca ideology were apparent in the Coricancha's sacred garden – a precious miniature landscape in which every kind of life known to the Incas was modelled in gold, silver and precious jewels. Butterflies, serpents, llamas, human beings and even the soil itself were all fashioned from these precious substances. They were the spiritual proto-types of earthly forms of life, protected by the divine emperor, who himself was considered to be the 'Son of the Sun'.

The powerful weather god Ilyap'a was prayed to for rain. He combined the sound of thunder with the power of thunderbolts and the flash of lightning. When the often torrential rains came, the Incas saw it as the god drawing water from the celestial river of the Milky Way which was then kept in a huge water jug by his sister, and only released when he shattered the vessel with a slingshot in the form of a lightning bolt. Thunder was the crack of his slingshot, and lightning the sparkle of his brilliant clothing as he advanced across the sky.

The third most important Inca deity was Mama Kilya, the moon goddess, the sister–wife of Inti, and mother of the Inca race. The relationship between these two gods served as a sacred prototype for brother–sister marriage practised by the Inca emperor. Mama Kilya was responsible for the passage of time and for regulating the many religious festivals of the ritual calendar. The Incas believed that during a lunar eclipse a great serpent or mountain lion was trying to devour Mama Kilya's celestial image, and so they made as much noise as possible in an attempt to scare the creature away. Mama Kilya's symbolic associations with Inca nobility mirrored those of her brother- husband Inti. Her image in the Coricancha was flanked by mummies of previous Inca queens or *Coyas*, and the shrine itself was covered in silver – the colour of the moon in the night sky.

Apart from this trilogy of sky gods, a host of lesser deities also figured in Inca religion. Among these was Cuichu, the rainbow, and a group of female supernatural beings – most notably Pacha Mama the earth-mother, and Mama Coca, the sea-mother.

Serving the Inca gods was an elaborate priesthood about which we know very little as they were targets for Spanish accusations of devil worship and paganism. In general the priesthood seems to have reflected Inca society, with the top level being closely related to the emperor. In Cuzco, at the time of the Spanish arrival, the high priest of Inti was Villac Umu – whose official title was 'slave of the Sun'. Lower down the social scale were those who made sacrifices, interpreted oracles and cured illness. Diviners predicted the future with maize grains or spiders which they kept in hollow human bones and then observed how they fell to the ground.

Most famous were the *acllas* or 'chosen women' – sometimes called the 'Virgins of the Sun'. Supervised by elder women, the *mama cunas* (i.e. 'mothers'), these young Inca maidens served the cult of Inti, tending the royal mummies of past emperors and queens as well as the present royal family. They were selected for their physical beauty and perfection at the age of ten and lived cloistered in convents called *aclla huasi.* Some prepared the clothing and food, and brewed the *chicha* beer that the Inca drank on state occasions. Others, taking a vow of chastity in honour of the Sun, had an important symbolic duty in guarding the sacred fire for the important Inti Raymi festival. The high priestess of these was a high-ranking noblewoman, symbolically regarded as the Sun god's wife. Some *acllas* were selected to be concubines for the emperor. These were also used on occasion as a tool of imperial policy – given by the emperor to foreign dignitaries with whom the Inca wished to form political marriage alliances.

SACRIFICE AND RITUAL

Sacrifice was an important act which accompanied every religious occasion from a grand official ceremony to private devotions. For the most part, sacrifices took the form of burnt offerings of vegetable foods, especially maize, but could also be coca leaves and pieces of clothing. They were often accompanied by the pouring of *chicha* beer onto the ground as an offering to Pacha Mama, the earth mother. Animals such as llamas and the ever-present guinea pigs were also frequent sacrifices. Llama sacrifice was especially important, as only certain kinds of the animals were considered suitable for a particular deity. Where white llamas were sacrificed to the Sun, brown llamas were offered to Viracocha, and multi-coloured ones to Ilyap'a. Sometimes small figurines of gold and silver were offered, hung on a temple wall or buried in the ground.

Less frequent, but most prized of all, were rituals of child sacrifice known as *capac hucha*, or 'royal obligation'. Such valuable offerings were made only on special occasions such as times of war or famine, and especially at the death of one emperor and the coronation of his successor. The victims were usually children, who were sometimes buried alive to ensure the new emperor's health and long life, and at other times were ritually strangled. Some two hundred children were sacrificed when a new emperor came to the throne. Inca priests recited prayers to Viracocha prior to such offerings: 'O Creator who gave life to all, since you said let there be day and night. Tell your son the Sun when the day breaks to come out in peace and safety, shine on all those who await you, let none be sick; keep everyone safe and sound.'

The ritual of *capac hucha* had a wider importance for Inca politics and ideology. These sacrifices embodied and integrated ideas of sacred time and space in the imperial Inca vision of the world. The ritual involved sending one or several children of outstanding beauty from every village in the empire to Cuzco. There they were honoured by the emperor and his priests, symbolically married, then led in procession around the great central plaza before starting the long journey back to their villages. On returning home, they were received with jubilation and thanksgiving and, after having been made drunk with *chicha*, they were buried alive at the site of a local *huaca*, usually the peak of a nearby mountain.

The rarity of human sacrifice among the Inca, compared for example with the Aztecs of Mexico, magnified the importance of such occasions, as did the nature of the two journeys made by the children. On the outward procession, they travelled along the system of royal roads, but on the return they followed the sacred straight (*ceque*) lines, ignoring geographical obstacles. The elders of the contributing villages were rewarded by the Inca for offering their children, and local ancestor spirits inhabiting their *huacas* also were honoured. The death of the child restored spiritual well-being and maintained the balance of obligations between the far-flung corners of empire and Cuzco. The symbolic marriages established a web of kin relations between villages, local rulers and the imperial court at Cuzco where they had taken place. The *capac hucha* ritual is a dramatic example of how the Incas imposed their ideas on a physical landscape, and converted these into religious rituals which reinforced political loyalties and the stability of the empire.

In recent years high altitude sacrifices in the form of frozen mummies have been found preserved by the cold on snowcapped Andean peaks and volcanoes. They are often accompanied by small human and animal figurines in gold, silver and coral-coloured sea shell, as well as by fine cloth and coca leaves. The figurines may be miniature versions of the gifts bestowed on adult couples at the beginning of married life. The eight- or nine-year-old Inca boy discovered in near perfect condition in 1954 on the summit of Mt Plomo, near Santiago in Chile, is the most famous, though in 1995 a teenage girl dressed in a red-and-white shawl was found on top of Mt Ampato, near Arequipa, in southern Peru.

For the Incas, the mummies of sacrificed children were but part of a religious practice that included the cult of the royal mummies. This in turn was but a development from the ancient Andean tradition of ancestor worship where even small villages venerated the mummies of their deified ancestors. The Inca adapted this to suit their imperial religion which regarded the emperor as the divine offspring of the Sun god Inti.

In Inca belief the emperor never died. While his body might cease to function, his spirit infused his mummified remains with life and was fortified by acts of worship and respect by his family and retainers. The cult of royal Inca mummies was associated with politics and privilege. The dead Inca's mummy was regularly washed, fed and clothed by his lineage group or *panaqa*, and often carried in ritual procession to 'visit' other dead Incas. All royal mummies attended state occasions, where, sitting in order of seniority, they added sanctity to the ruling order and authority to the living emperor.

THREE

Inca Society

Inca society was hierarchical and strictly organized. This was its strength and its weakness. At the top was the emperor, the *Sapa* (unique) Inca, who ruled by divine right as the 'son of the Sun'. Worshipped as a living god, his official wife was his full-blooded sister, known as the *Coya*. The practice of marrying a sister was restricted to the emperor and was enshrined in mythology by the Sun god Inti having married his sister the Moon goddess Mama Kilya. As absolute ruler of the world, the Inca emperor also had a harem of concubines made up of the most beautiful young women from across the empire, the *acllas* or 'chosen women'. Their royal offspring were given positions of power and influence in Inca society. The male descendants of every emperor formed a royal *ayllu* or *panaqa* whose responsibility it was to serve the emperor and protect his wealth and estates. This inner circle of educated and talented men were those from whom were chosen the empire's top administrators.

As a divine being, upon whose well-being the fate of the empire depended, the emperor was surrounded by elaborate rituals and restrictions. His food, drink and clothing were specially prepared by the *acllas* and *mama cunas*. Every scrap of uneaten food, every item of worn clothing, and even hairs from his head and nail clippings were gathered up and ceremonially burnt. This was to prevent the possibility of sorcery where illness or disaster could be conjured up with something which had come from, or been in contact with, the living god's body.

Access to the emperor's presence was strictly controlled. Such was the *Sapa* Inca's lordly status that all who sought an audience with him could approach only after taking off their sandals and carrying a symbolic burden on their backs. Seeing the god-emperor face to face was a great honour and was restricted to important visitors. Most of those admitted into the royal presence never saw the emperor as they were separated from him by a screen, thereby maintaining the mystique and social distance between ruler and ruled.

Whatever the social status of his visitors, the 'son of the Sun' was always presented appropriately, sitting on a low wooden bench on top of a raised platform – the combined elements being called an *usnu* or throne. Here he sat, dressed in finely woven cloth, adorned with earrings of gold and silver, and holding his ceremonial mace. On his forehead he wore the most important badge of office – a fringe of red tassels sprouting from a number of small golden tubes suspended from a multi-coloured braid wrapped around his head.

When an Inca emperor died, it was believed that only his body had ceased to function – his spirit lived on and had to be treated with respect. The physical remains were preserved and the royal mummy placed in his palace which now became a mausoleum. There he continued to 'live' in familiar surroundings. Sacrifices were made to him, and he was dressed, washed, 'fed' and waited upon by servants just as he had been in life. Carried on a special litter, he made grand visits to the mummies of other deceased emperors, or those friends who had outlived him. These activities illustrate not just how different were Inca ideas of life and death from modern western views, but also show the close connections between religion and politics. The dead emperor's palaces, estates and wealth continued to be his property but were now administered by his *panaqa* (with the exception of the newly crowned emperor). The members of the *panaqa* were charged with perpetuating the dead emperor's memory and achievements through his royal cult. By so doing they also ensured their own privileged positions, becoming influential political factions in the power plays of imperial Inca society.

Beneath the *Sapa* Inca came the nobility, divided between the higher class – itself split into two kinds, 'Incas by blood' and 'Incas by privilege', and the lower class called the *curacas*. Of the two kinds of higher-class Incas the most powerful were the hereditary aristocracy. They belonged to eleven royal *ayllus*. However, in the early days of Inca expansion the numbers of full-blooded Inca nobles had proved insufficient to fill all the new offices of state. The

Emperor Pachacuti ingeniously solved the problem by extending the privileges of Inca status to able and gifted individuals who spoke Quechua. They were often added to the imperial retinue to carry out a specific task, and if they served the emperor well they could expect to be amply rewarded. These individuals were extremely loyal as they owed their position solely to the emperor. Also, as they were often appointed on merit, they could be removed at any time if they failed in their duties.

There were also the so-called *yana* or servant lords – those in personal service to the emperor who had been elevated to high status. The personal nature of such appointments strengthened the emperor's hand again by creating strong individual loyalties between servant and lord, rewarding the trustworthy, and keeping the other grades of lords on their toes. Between them these two levels of Inca aristocracy ruled the empire, and were rewarded by being allowed to wear insignia similar to those of the emperor – such as coloured headbands and braids and the large earplugs which led to the Spanish calling them *orejones* (big ears).

Below this two-tiered ruling class were the *curacas* who formed the lower echelons of Inca nobility. These individuals filled most of the administrative offices of government and also connected the imperial Inca bureaucracy with the older pre-Inca traditions of social obligations and ancestor worship. Although the native rulers of conquered peoples could become *curacas*, many were the hereditary chiefs of local communities. There were two *curacas* for each Inca *ayllu* – one for each of the two moieties, the symbolic halves into which traditional Andean societies were divided and which the Inca incorporated into their own social organization.

Ayllus were the bedrock of Andean society and remain so today. Essentially they are a group of related individuals and families who share their labour, lands and herds. Each *ayllu* is composed of lineages which belong either to the upper or lower moiety, and membership is traced through female lines for women and male lines for men. *Ayllus* also hold rights to water, both to springs and lakes, as well as the canals which transport it.

An *ayllu*'s *curacas* were intermediaries between their people and the spirit world, as traditionally each *ayllu* had a founding ancestor. During Inca times, these were integrated into the official hierarchy of ancestors at whose summit was the living emperor, his mummified predecessors, and the Sun god Inti.

On an everyday basis, *curacas* managed the *ayllu*'s resources. They oversaw the calendar of agricultural activities, managed disputes over land and water, and provided large quantities of *chicha* beer for ceremonial occasions. In return, the men and women of the *ayllu* tilled the *curacas*' lands, gathered their crops, tended their herds and made their woven clothes. *Curacas* were organized in a decimal system, each with a different title, according to how many people they were responsible for. A *pacaka koraka* was a chief of 100 people, a *waranqa* was chief of 1,000, and a *hono koraka* was chief of 10,000.

As the Inca armies conquered new areas, so the empire included large strips of coastal desert and the cities of its oasis-like river valleys. This meant that new and different kinds of specialists had to be incorporated into the empire. These included merchants who had plied their trades long before the Incas came to power. The most famous of these were the traders from the important city of Chincha. According to some accounts there were some 6,000 of these merchants who regularly traded overland to Cuzco and the Lake Titicaca region where they obtained copper. Returning to the coast they then sailed their ocean-going rafts north to Ecuador, where they exchanged the metal for the red-coloured spondylus shell known as *mullu*. The religious importance of spondylus had been long established in the Andes, and control of its trade added significantly to Inca wealth and prestige.

Apart from these specialized groups who lived and worked beyond the highlands, the lower echelons of Inca society were composed of several kinds of commoners. Artisans, though working for the state, nevertheless enjoyed a privileged position in Inca society. Those who worked in gold and silver were freed from having to give their labour and time to the empire's agricultural and military workforce. In newly conquered areas such specialists were moved wholesale either to Cuzco or other important Inca cities. Metalworkers, textile workers and master potters from the farthest reaches of the empire were thus incorporated into Inca society.

The mass of unskilled people however had only their physical labour to offer. The *hatun runa*, or adult men, were farmers and herders, who grew maize and potatoes and looked after the flocks of llama, alpaca and vicuña. They were the backbone of the labour force, organized during the reign of Inca Tupac Yupanqui into units of 10, 100, 1,000 and 10,000. Below them, at the very bottom of Inca society, were the piña or prisoners-of-war.

The success of Inca society depended to a great extent on the ability of bureaucrats to record the details of the empire and thus organize it more efficiently. Yet, uniquely among the world's great civilizations, neither the Incas nor their predecessors possessed writing. This problem was solved with typical ingenuity by developing a communication system which fulfilled the same purposes as writing but was linked to the oral traditions of Andean society and which had appeared first in the earlier Wari culture. This was the *quipu*, a series of knotted strings, of which over 400 have survived. Some *quipus* were more than ten feet long with 2,000 individual strings. Although widely believed to have been used mainly for keeping numbers of llama flocks, some *quipus* may have recorded mathematical and astronomical information, and possibly also preserved prayers, genealogical information, and perhaps even songs and plays. This information was gathered and 'read' by the *quipu camayoc* – the 'Keepers of the *quipu*' – who were a human library of Inca knowledge and traditions.

Detailed knowledge of the *quipu* disappeared after the Spanish conquest. The Inca government had supported the *quipu camayoc* as specialist occupations and when it collapsed they were no longer required. In addition, Spanish (both spoken and written) became the new language of power. The intricate secret code of the *quipu* died with the last *quipu camayoc*, though modern investigations suggest that information was recorded by varying the type, colour and position of knots on subsidiary strings suspended from the main cord.

EVERYDAY LIFE

The details kept on the *quipu* recorded the achievements of a highly regimented society of men, women and children, who had strictly defined roles as farmers, artisans, bureaucrats and priests. Although daily existence could vary greatly according to an individual's position in society, some features of life in the empire were the same for everyone.

Inca society was organized around work. So important was this that the Incas did not keep track of their individual ages. Instead, everyone was classified according to their physical strength and condition and their ability to undertake different kinds of activities. Children between the ages of five and nine were called 'those who played', though boys still helped their parents and girls learned to sew. Between nine and twelve, older boys graduated to hunting birds while girls picked flowers and dyed cloth. It was from this age group that the empire's most beautiful girls were chosen to be the human sacrifices known as *capac hucha*. Between roughly eighteen and twenty years old the young men took on the responsibility of guarding the llama and alpaca flocks and becoming the imperial messengers or *chasqui*. At the same time, girls could now find themselves dedicated to the Sun as *acllas*. A commoner's main work in life as a farmer or herder, weaver or mother, took place between the ages of twenty-five and fifty. In recognition of increasing age only light work was done between sixty and seventy, and once over eighty little or nothing was expected of those called the 'old deaf ones'.

This dedication to hard physical work characterized daily life for most Inca men. Although women helped their husbands in the fields at harvest-time, the home was the centre of their life. Here they prepared food, and spent much time in spinning and weaving the family's wool and cotton clothing. Men wore a long sleeveless tunic over a breechclout, and a large cloak in bad weather. On their husband's everyday clothes wives kept decoration to a minimum, though around the waist a row of small squares with internal designs may have communicated information of social or ethnic importance. Men also carried a small bag in which they kept coca leaves, small tools and any magical charms they needed. They kept their hair cut and wore sandals made from untanned llama skin.

Inca women dressed in a similarly conservative style. They wore long dresses made of rectangular pieces of cloth fastened at the shoulder with copper, silver or gold pins. A sash around the waist was decorated with similar square designs as was found in men's tunics. They wore their hair long and parted in the middle though might also wrap it with a woven braid. As might be expected in a large multi-ethnic society, clothing and hairstyles varied from one part of the empire to another, depending on the tribal identities of each region.

All members of the aristocracy wore jewellery. Noble men were recognizable by their large ear-plugs which could be made from wood, gold or silver. Bracelets and shiny metal chest ornaments also were worn by the higher class. For noble women bodily decoration was simpler. They were permitted only to wear necklaces of shell beads and the pins that fastened their clothing.

Marriage was an important institution for the Incas,

for whom it had strong ritual and economic as well as social importance. When a woman or man wished to marry they had to choose a partner from the opposite moiety in their *ayllu*, as marriage beyond the community was prohibited. The best marriage partners were those with the largest families because, as everyone was born with rights to labour, land and water, each relative brought in wealth in one way or another.

Inca men of royal blood were permitted to marry their half-sisters, perhaps as a gesture from the emperor who always took one of his sisters as his principal wife. Those who distinguished themselves in the emperor's service might be rewarded with a gift of other women. The more wives a man had the more his wealth and prestige was seen to be.

For the common man, however, one wife was all he could usually afford. When he married he was recognized as a full adult member of the community and took on the full range of duties and obligations expected of him. In recognition of this, the newly wed couple were given enough land for a house and to support themselves. As the family grew so the village authorities provided more land.

Despite differences between social classes, the Incas and their subject peoples lived the same kind of life when it came to such everyday activities as eating and drinking. The Andes are one of the world's great centres of plant domestication, and this had a profound effect on the mainly vegetable diet of its peoples. Because of the vertical arrangement of different ecological areas, different food plants from different altitudes could be exchanged and traded across comparatively short distances. This was a key feature of pre-Inca societies and now became an important characteristic of Inca life.

In the high valleys many varieties of potato were grown as the staple food, as was the grain quinoa whose leaves were boiled like spinach. At lower altitudes maize replaced the potato, and was supplemented by tarwi (another grain), roqoto (a chile pepper), and squash. From the even lower hotter valleys came different chiles, the sweet root acira, gourds, and the sacred coca leaf.

Further variety in the Andean diet was offered by peanuts, sweet potatoes, tomatoes, beans, sweet manioc, and avocados. Less often, roasted insect larvae and the fruits of several kinds of cactus were also eaten. Although heavily dependent on vegetables, meat also figured in the Inca diet. In addition to game animals such as deer and guanaco, as well as fish, domestic animals were also eaten. Llamas, ducks and the ubiquitous household guinea pigs were readily available in Inca times as they still are today throughout the Andes.

Although there was a tremendous variety in their diet the Incas usually ate their food in the form of stews and soups, flavoured with various herbs and chiles. Such dishes included *locro,* a meat or fish stew with potatoes, vegetables and chiles, and *motepatasca,* maize cooked with herbs and chiles. As elsewhere in the Americas, maize was an incredibly versatile food. It could be boiled, toasted, made into popcorn, and also steamed or baked as a kind of maize bread. Llama meat, potatoes and ocas were frequently dried and stored. Although they had no distilled alcohol, the Inca did make *chicha* beer from a variety of plants such as maize and quinoa. Consumed as an everyday beverage, it was drunk to excess only on religious occasions. Also important as a stimulant

47

rather than a food was the coca leaf which deadened feelings of hunger and thirst and was reportedly good for the teeth.

The Incas ordinarily ate twice a day, in the morning and afternoon with everyone sitting on the ground and the women serving their husbands from the cooking pots. On grander occasions, like public banquets, each family brought its own food and sat in two rows with the presiding dignitary seated on a stool at their head. When drinking someone's health a man would take two cups of *chicha* to the man he wished to toast. After handing over one cup the two men would drink together. At the greatest Inca festival of all, the Inti Raymi celebrations in honour of the Sun god, participants prepared themselves by fasting for three days on a meagre diet of raw white maize, a few herbs and water. The night before the feast the Inca priests prepared the llamas for sacrifice and gathered together many kinds of food as offerings to the sun. The *acllas* made huge quantities of maize dough called *çancu* which they shaped into little round loaves. This was a sacred food eaten only on important occasions.

Every aspect of daily life was subject to government control. There were rules and regulations for everyone and every occasion. Andean peoples, today as in the past, are deeply conservative, and the Incas took advantage of this by making humility and respect for authority the cornerstones of social behaviour. They gave their legal system the force of religion by regarding civil disobedience not only a social offence but also as sacrilege towards the god-emperor. For even the smallest offences punishments were harsh. These included hanging, stoning, and being pushed off cliffs. Those accused of treason were thrown into an underground cavern filled with pumas and snakes. Despite such severity, the Incas recognized a difference between the social class of the offender as well as the offence. The educated upper classes were punished more severely than commoners as they were expected to know and behave better. Adultery meant death to a noble whereas a commoner suffered only torture.

At the end of life, the Incas marked death with special ceremonies during which the relatives wore black and women cut their hair. Food was served to all who attended and the mourning rituals could continue for up to a year if the deceased had been of noble birth. Some of the dead person's belongings were ceremonially burnt and then the body and remaining goods were wrapped in cloth and buried. When a member of the aristocracy died the funerals were on a grander scale and sometimes secondary wives and servants might be killed so as to accompany their master. Regular offerings of food and drink were made at the tomb by the dead person's relatives, perhaps in imitation of similar but more elaborate rituals which surrounded the royal mummies of dead emperors. However, the honouring of the dead in this way was also part of the rituals of the age-old tradition of ancestor worship in the Andes.

FOUR

The Quest for Empire

A HISTORY OF EMPIRE

In the early days, before about AD 1400, little had distinguished the Incas from many other small Andean groups living in the vicinity of the Valley of Cuzco. Charismatic war leaders fought small-scale battles in attempts at local supremacy, and fortunes ebbed and flowed. Little is known for certain about this period, partly due to the lack of indigenous written records. Also, in later years, the increasingly powerful Inca rulers rewrote their humble origins with a mix of mythology and propaganda, further confusing the picture. What does seems certain is that some time before 1438 a powerful people known as the Chanca had attacked and defeated the Quechuas, a culture allied to the Incas to the northwest of Cuzco. Seeking to expand their territory, the Chancas cast an envious eye on the fertile Cuzco valley but bided their time until the Inca leader, Viracocha Inca, was an old man.

When the Chanca finally attacked, many Inca nobles panicked and persuaded the elderly Viracocha Inca to flee Cuzco and take refuge in a nearby fortress. Some of his generals, together with two of his sons, Yupanqui and Roca, refused to abandon the city and set about fortifying it instead. The Chanca laid seige but Inca resolve held, with Yupanqui crying out that even the stones on the battlefield were turning into men to help them. The Chanca attack was finally repulsed and the magical stones collected and put into the city's shrines. In a later battle the Incas again defeated the Chancas and with this victory the tables were finally turned. In the days that followed Yupanqui had himself crowned as the new Inca ruler at which time he took the name Pachacuti (i.e. cataclysm).

This is the official version of events, yet it almost certainly conceals a more complicated story. Viracocha's retreat and Yupanqui's victory were probably surrounded by political intrigues between different factions of Inca society. The war with the Chancas also was more likely to have been a long drawn-out affair, later reduced to one heroic stand at the siege of Cuzco. Nevertheless, it was Pachacuti and his supporters who emerged victorious and began on the path to empire.

Pachacuti was an unusually talented man. Not only was he a brilliant general but also a great administrator. The Inca Empire was his vision and creation. He was also fortunate to have a son, Tupac Yupanqui, who matched this brilliance. Father and son together organized military campaigns throughout the Andes, extending the boundaries of Tawantinsuyu north into modern Ecuador, and south into Argentina and Chile.

The Inca armies swept through neighbouring Andean kingdoms and then down onto the south coast of Peru. Some areas submitted quickly while others offered stiff resistance, but always the size and efficiency of the Inca armies proved irresistible. Pachacuti was also careful not to anger his former enemies the Chanca and allowed them to conquer areas around Lake Titicaca on his behalf. Attention then moved to the north where Pachacuti's generals and allies conquered many local tribes. Conquest, however, was always a temporary affair as unrest often flared in subjugated areas. Local politics and jealousies of conquered peoples towards the growing power of the Incas led to a revolt in the area of Lake Titicaca. Pachacuti was forced to lead an army in person where he scored a bloody victory and took the opportunity to conquer the Lupaca kingdom and even to raid the southern and eastern shores of the lake.

As time went on Pachacuti increasingly handed over control of the armies to his son and eventual heir, Tupac Yupanqui, while he concentrated on overhauling the empire's administration. Pachacuti also began a massive project to rebuild Cuzco and transform it into an imperial capital.

Tupac Yupanqui took his father's armies north-wards once again. He reinforced the areas won previously then pushed the imperial frontier towards Quito. He then marched west, conquering the land between the Andes and the Ecuadorian coast around the town of Manta, stopping only long enough, according to one source, to voyage out into the Pacific on one of the large sea- going balsa-wood rafts used by the seafaring traders of the area. His next decisive move was to outmanoeuvre and defeat the last great independent kingdom of Peru – the Chimú empire of the north coast. Tupac outflanked the Chimú, conquered their great city of Chan Chan, and pushed south along the shores of the Pacific, conquering all the towns as far as the central coast of Peru. On returning to Cuzco, he turned his attention to the southernmost valleys of Peru, bringing them into the empire. It was for such brilliant military victories that Tupac Yupanqui has been called the Alexander the Great of South America.

Around 1471, the elderly Pachacuti finally handed over the red tassle of imperial power to his son after a reign of thirty-three years. Almost immediately after having been crowned Sapa Inca, Tupac launched a new offensive eastwards into the tropical rainforests. No sooner had Tupac disappeared into the jungle than rumours of his defeat by forest

Indians brought an uprising by the Lupaca and Colla peoples around Lake Titicaca. The new emperor turned back immediately and made his way south. Although the rebels had taken refuge in a fortified rock-summit they were overwhelmed by the imperial forces and the rebellion was crushed.

As tireless as ever, Tupac then invaded the highlands of modern Bolivia, and received the submission of peoples who lived in what is today North-west Argentina. Driven by visions of himself as master of the known world, Tupac advanced southwest into Chile across the Atacama desert. He established the southern boundary of the empire by the banks of the River Maule. Most of Tupac's remaining rule was taken up with refining and consolidating his father's reorganization of the empire. In just over fifty years, and with astonishing speed, the two men had created the largest empire ever seen in the Americas.

Tupac had reigned for twenty-two years when he died in 1493 and was succeeded by his son, Huayna Capac. The new emperor's rule was a time of great upheaval in the Andean world. The Incas seemed forever to be putting down revolts and, on one memorable occasion, they had to repulse an invasion of the empire's south-eastern border by the Chiriguano Indians from Argentina. The Chiriguano brought with them a strange hostage – the Spaniard Alejo García who had been captured on South America's Atlantic coast. García was the first and only European to see the Inca Empire at the height of its power. Huayna Capac pushed back the invaders but never defeated them. His northern campaigns added parts of Ecuador's coast to the empire, and he also established the empire's northern boundary at the Ancasmayo river near what is today the border between Ecuador and Colombia.

Huayna Capac died unexpectedly in somewhat mysterious circumstances in 1527. Just before his death he heard news of strangers from the sea who had stopped briefly at the northern port of Tumbez. This was the eventual conquereor of the Inca empire, Francisco Pizarro, on an earlier voyage of exploration. In fact it may have been that Huayna Capac's death was caused by a European disease which spread from the northern part of South

America through the Amazon and up to Quito long before Europeans themselves arrived in Peru. Whatever the cause, Huayna Capac's death was so swift that he had no time to announce his successor. This failure highlighted an inherent weakness in Inca rulership, where courtly intrigues and no firm rules of succession often created confusion. For the next five years, between 1527 and 1532, a disastrous civil war tore apart the empire of the Sun.

Although it seems as if Huayna Capac's official son Huascar should have taken the throne, the realities were more complicated. While Huascar was recognized immediately by the nobility and priesthood in Cuzco, another son by one of the dead emperor's concubines in Quito challenged for the throne. This son, called Atahualpa, at first announced himself governor of Quito in Huascar's name, but then become bolder, claiming that their father Huayna Capac had split the empire into two parts and that he was assuming the lordship of the northern half.

Although Huascar had official backing and held most of the empire, Atahualpa had been left in command of most of the army and two of Huayna Capac's most seasoned generals, Quisquis and Chalcuchima. Emboldened by these strokes of luck, Atahualpa's ambition soon grew to the point where he abandoned the idea of ruling half the empire and instead began campaigning against Huascar. The issue of legitimacy was to be decided by force of arms. Atahualpa's generals outwitted and outfought Huascar's army, captured the emperor, and massacred the leading members of his *panaqa*. It was in the northern town of Cajamarca that Atahualpa finally received news of his total victory. Unfortunately this was accompanied by the reappearance of strangers – the Spanish conquistadors of Francisco Pizarro.

ORGANIZATION OF EMPIRE

The success of the Incas was due to several factors. Not only were Pachacuti and Tupac Yupanqui gifted military commanders, but their skills extended to the administration of what was in effect a vast and sprawling multi-cultural empire. Organizing a mosaic of ethnic groups, languages and religious traditions was a kind of social engineering at which these two leaders excelled and upon which consolidation of military victories depended.

The Inca empire was first and foremost Pre-Columbian America's largest conquest power. The Incas waged war for political and ideological reasons as well as for profit. Unlike the Maya or Aztecs of Mexico, Inca military strategy aimed to increase the empire's size and add to the prestige and wealth of the Sun god and his chosen people, rather than to acquire prisoners-of-war for sacrifice. The Incas believed warfare was a religious duty that nevertheless greatly benefitted the royal family.

These benefits and Inca politics seem to have driven the empire forward. When an emperor died the empire was bequeathed to his successor, but the income from the lands he had conquered was retained by his *panaqa* or male descendants. The new emperor thus had to acquire his own lands and wealth through renewed conquest, which in turn became the source of wealth for his *panaqa* when he died. Apart from the ambitions of these royal pressure groups to guarantee their own positions, the Inca state itself needed ever greater quantities of goods. As the empire expanded, so did the number of local lords whose continued loyalty to the Incas had to be bought with regular gifts of food, clothing, women, gold and silver. The Incas had to conquer new lands to increase their wealth and so stabilize the empire.

Although the *Sapa* Inca maintained a royal body-guard of professional warriors, the Inca army itself was composed mainly of levies from all able-bodied male citizens. These men were peasant farmers whose labour tax or *mita* was rendered as periods of military service. They were reinforced by special units such as archers from the tropical rainforests and spear-throwers from the coast. Apart from these groups, the majority of Inca warriors were no better equipped than their enemies. They wore quilted cotton tunics and fought with spears, slings, battle-axes and war-clubs. War-drums were made of human skin and some warriors wore necklaces of human teeth. Although marching discipline was strict, battlefield tactics were primitive. The imperial Inca armies usually relied on superior numbers to

61

overwhelm their opponents. Often it was the Inca psychology of war and speed of movement which intimidated their enemies, with large numbers of soldiers being moved quickly and efficiently over the difficult Andean terrain along the imperial roads.

Pachacuti and Tupac Yupanqui were outstanding generals, but they also understood the value of religion and diplomacy among the politically divided, conservative and superstitious peoples of the Andes. Once they decided on an area to conquer they invited the native leaders to join the empire peacefully and share in the privileges and benefits of Inca power. Many accepted the offer. Tupac Yupanqui's astonishing conquests are thought to have been due in large part to his shrewd use of diplomacy. If this tactic failed the Inca armies were marched to a nearby strategic point and last-minute offers were made. If these were rejected then the Inca gods were invoked and their priests read the signs of entrails of sacrificed llamas. If the auguries were good then fighting began.

The empire that these tactics won for the Incas was called Tawantinsuyu – 'the land of the four quarters'. With the capital of Cuzco at its centre, the four quarters encompassed the whole known world. Collasuyu was the largest quarter and stretched over the mountains and coast to the south, Antisuyu was the smallest and was home to the tropical forest-dwelling Indians of the north-east, Cuntisuyu included all areas to the south-west, and Chinchasuyu incorporated the extensive mountains and coasts of the northern Andes. Each quarter or *suyu* was governed by a royal prefect and was divided into provinces. These were under the control of an imperial governor, and were in turn divided into two or three sections composed of *ayllus*. This system was a tribute to the Inca genius for organizing a variety of landscapes, peoples, religions and languages.

By mobilizing their vast resources of manpower the Incas transformed whole valleys by large-scale terracing, roadbuilding, bridge construction and hydraulic engineering, such as the straightening or canalization of the Vilcanota (Urubamba) river. Such projects also possessed religious and ideological dimensions. Many of the impressive agricultural terraces etched into the sides of mountains produced maize, not for food, but for the manufacture of vast quantities of *chicha* beer which were given 'free' to the people during the many religious festivals.

The arteries of this empire of perhaps 10–20 million people were the vast system of imperial roads. Planned by Inca engineers, at least 30,000 km of roads were built and maintained by local people through whose territory sections of the roads passed. In the highlands, an Inca road could be a narrow path hewn from the living rock and just wide enough for a man and his llamas to pass. These roads crossed the rivers and gorges which characterize this region by sophisticated suspension bridges. Some of these were so large that the Spanish were able to race on horseback across them. On the coast, where construction was easier, roads could be wide avenues with several lanes serving as ceremonial approaches to important towns. Dotted along these roads at regular intervals were innumerable way-stations and storehouses called *tambos* in which were kept supplies of food, drink, weapons and clothing.

Inca roads were not for everyone. Only those on official business, the imperial runners or *chasqui*, and the emperor and his armies could use them. *Chasqui* are said to have been able to run in relays up to 250 km a day, delivering messages between distant parts of the empire often faster than the modern postal systems of today.

Beyond their heartland, in newly conquered areas, the Incas founded administrative centres imposed onto the subject peoples. As with monumental structures nearer home, such as Ollantaytambo and Sacsayhuaman, huge blocks of stone were carved out of mountainside quarries and dragged along ramps to their place of use. Here they were carved and hammered and fitted together ingeniously without mortar in the distinctive polygonal Inca style. This was an impressive and pyschologically intimidating building style but also had its practical side. When earthquakes rocked the land, the stones would rise up then settle back into their original positions. Later colonial Spanish buildings built of brick and mortar often collapsed completely with disastrous consequences. Built with the aid of miniature models and the *quipu*, these provincial Inca capitals were designed as miniature versions of Cuzco.

One such city was Huánuco Pampa, north-west of Cuzco. Typically it had only a small permanent population of Inca administrators to control the local people. Yet its size, some four thousand buildings spread over 200 ha, suggests that several thousand people could be housed during the elaborate festivities which were held there.

As with Cuzco, Huánuco Pampa was built around a great plaza. Two now headless carved stone pumas adorn the entrance to the ceremonial throne or usnu. On all sides are the remains of buildings which include a palace built for Inca Tupac Yupanqui, an area for cooking and feasting, and an *aclla huasi* where the 'chosen women' brewed *chicha* beer and made clothing for local Inca officials and as gifts which the emperor gave as signs of royal favour on ceremonial occasions. The land around Huánuco Pampa was also put to good use, with some five hundred storehouses strategically located for ventilation and arranged in neat rows. They originally contained stockpiles of vegetables, such as maize, tubers and potatoes. The artificial nature of these centres – located for administrative purposes rather than at natural locations for local peoples – meant that when the Spanish arrived they were abandoned virtually overnight.

Similarly specialized was the famous mountain-top city of Machu Picchu. Rediscovered only in 1911, the importance of this city lies in its superb preservation. It was never discovered, and therefore never damaged, by the Spaniards. Its spectacular location, covering 100 acres on a spur encircled by the sacred Vilcanota river, suggests it lay at the heart of Inca sacred geography. It was built originally by Pachacuti possibly as a fortress though later, as the empire moved on, it became his royal estate. The quality of the architecture and workmanship is impressive, as seen in the elaborate terraces that surround the site and the intricate system of water channels and fountains that still work today. Also built of fine masonry are such buildings as the semi-circular 'observatory' which encloses a white stone beneath which is a cave known as the 'Royal Mausoleum'. These buildings, along with the carved-stone block of the Intihuatana (or 'hitching post of the sun'), indicate the religious nature of the city at least in its later days.

As a masterstroke of political organization, the Incas innovated a system whereby local populations were transferred from one place to another. These people were called *mitmaq*, and by moving thousands of families like pieces on a giant chessboard, the Incas hoped to secure their borders, ensure stability, and remove the focus of any potential revolt. These colonists were sometimes moved thousands of miles from their own villages and yet retained their native dress and remained under the authority of their own local chiefs. They propagated Inca values and fostered the adoption of the official language of Quechua. On occasion there was a straightforward exchange whereby a troublesome population was removed wholesale to an area further within the empire where they could be more easily controlled, while that region's original population became colonists in the evacuated area.

Money was unknown in Tawantinsuyu. Food, clothing, housing and other necessities of life were provided by local *ayllus* under strict government control. Instead of paying taxes in money, the empire's varied peoples paid tribute in goods and services, notably the labour tax known as the *mita*. Unless excused by the emperor, all able-bodied men had to give their time to the *mita*, which could be for varying lengths of time and include such work as building bridges, maintaining roads or serving in the army.

There were different kinds of *mita* service. Commoners, both men and women, were expected to work in the fields as a kind of agricultural taxation. As the empire grew and newly conquered lands were added, so the agricultural duties of *mita* workers were divided into three kinds. First to be cultivated was that portion of land allotted to religion – the Inca gods, local deities and *huacas*. The harvest from this land supported the priests and their helpers and was also stored to provide food and drink on religious occasions. Next to be worked was land which belonged to the emperor himself, and whose yields supported the aristocracy in Cuzco, fed the armies and was used for other official purposes. The third and last kind of land to be cared for was that which belonged to the local community. This was distributed to individual households by the local *curaca* and, as we have seen, varied according to the number of family members.

It was due to the huge resources of manpower which the Incas could mobilize with the *mita* that

69

enabled them to transform the Andean landscape. The skills of imperial engineers together with the massed *mita* labour force built an integrated system of roads, storehouses, canals, bridges, fortresses and towns, and maintained them. The sheer scale of this achievement is still visible in the vast terraces which span large areas of the Andes.

CUZCO, HEART OF THE EMPIRE

All roads in Tawantinsuyu led to Cuzco. Surrounded by the ice-capped folds of the Andes, this great city was the sacred heart of the empire as well as the focus of religious and political activity. It was here, in the great palaces and temples, that the *Sapa* Inca and his royal court resided, and where all the great decisions of state were made. Cuzco was not just a place, but also the embodiment of Inca myth, history and spiritual identity. As the place where earth, sky and rivers met, it was the empire's most important *huaca* – the centre of the universe.

Rebuilt on a grand scale by Pachacuti, Cuzco was laid out (according to some accounts) in the shape of a

Plan of Cuzco

giant puma, the predatory feline adopted by the Inca as a royal icon and symbol. Even today, there is a part of the city called *Puma Chupan*, 'the puma's tail'. The fierce 'head' was formed by the temple-fortress of Sacsayhuaman overlooking the city, and whose massive zig-zag walls may have been seen as the snarling jaws of the great cat. Within the body of the puma, and following ancient Andean tradition, Cuzco and its royal lineages were divided into two sacred halves or moieties, upper or *hanan* Cuzco occupying the space of the front part of the puma, and lower or *hurin* Cuzco situated in the beast's hindquarters. The city was located at the confluence of three rivers. Such places, where rivers or paths meet, were and still are regarded by Andean peoples as places of spiritual balance.

The city housed temples, palaces and shrines – all built of the finest quality masonry. The most important of these was the Coricancha or 'House of the Sun', whose inner walls were covered with sheets of solid gold. Flanked by the palace-mausoleums of earlier emperors, the heart of the city was an enormous plaza dominated by a ceremonial platform – the centre of creation. From here, the living emperor viewed the magnificent rituals on state occasions. Ideas of myth and sacred landscape were also important, as the floor of the great plaza was covered with sand brought up from the Pacific coast. This was a symbolic statement of the far-reaching power of the *Sapa* Inca, and linked Cuzco with the sea as the 'mother of fertility'. Access to the Valley of Cuzco was restricted, and the city's narrow streets and high-walled buildings seem to have been an architectural expression of the hierarchical nature of Inca society.

Cuzco was the mirror of heaven – its layout, monumental buildings and royal inhabitants were all organized by the ideas of religion and ideology. As we have seen, these organizing principles took the form of the forty-one sacred lines or *ceques* which radiated from the Coricancha. Criss-crossing the city, the *ceques* stretched out beyond the horizon, imposing order and meaning on the everyday and spiritual lives of the people. They seem also to have been associated with the straightness of both the imperial roads and the *quipu* knotted strings – each of which in their own way also imposed order and structure on the empire.

73

FIVE

The Spanish Conquest

The Spanish conquistador Francisco Pizarro was a tough and experienced soldier. He was already in his fifties when he first heard rumours of a land rich in gold in Panama in 1524. Three years later in 1527 he sailed south to explore the Pacific coast of South America and stumbled across an ocean-going balsa-wood raft off the coast of Ecuador. It was laden with gold and finely woven cloth. After many hardships and a mutiny, Pizarro joined forces with Bartolome Ruiz and together they sailed south from Ecuador to Peru. During the voyage they saw more seaborne rafts and observed many large towns dotted along the coast. Pizarro was convinced that the rumours he had heard were true, and that he could repeat the fabulous discoveries of Hernan Cortes in Mexico in 1519. He returned to Panama and from there made his way to Spain to raise money and obtain royal approval for a new expedition. In January 1531 he again set sail from Panama, this time with 180 men and 37 horses. He landed by mistake on the coast of Ecuador from where it took him a full year to arrive at the edge of the Inca Empire in Easter 1532.

As fate would have it, Pizarro found the Inca Empire wracked by years of civil war. The conflict had just been won by Atahualpa whose generals had recently defeated Huascar's army and captured the emperor. At the same time as Pizarro landed on the north coast, Atahualpa was moving south along the Andes from his base in Quito and had encamped in the highland city of Cajamarca. Hearing of the bitter power struggle, Pizarro planned to take advantage of the chaos it had produced.

In September 1532, Pizarro advanced with his small army into the heart of the Inca Empire. At Cajamarca the two forces finally met and the Spaniards were dismayed to see that the Inca army was about 30,000 strong. Pizarro immediately sent an embassy to the Inca Emperor, who, it is reported, took much interest in the Spaniards' horses. Atahualpa invited the Spaniards to stay at Cajamarca and promised to visit them in person the next day. That evening the Spaniards discussed their precarious situation. They decided to gamble everything on one audacious move: to ambush and capture Atahualpa.

The next day, Saturday 16 November 1532, Pizarro hid his soldiers and cavalry in the buildings of the town. They waited all day until, in the afternoon, the *Sapa* Inca approached the town surrounded by thousands of soldiers. They filled the plain outside Cajamarca like a human sea – resplendent in brightly coloured clothing and headdresses of flashing gold and silver. At sunset, the emperor entered the town square with 6,000 unarmed men. He saw no one and called out. Pizarro's Dominican priest, Vicente de Valverde, approached together with the expedition's boy interpreter. Atahualpa demanded the Spaniards give back everything they had stolen since their arrival. In response Valverde started to read the 'Requirement' – an account of the holy doctrine which the Spanish were obliged to read to any enemy before they resorted to violence. Atahualpa asked to see the book and examined it carefully, fingering page after page. Having never seen writing before, it remained a mystery to him. Finally, he threw it to the ground in disgust.

The critical moment had arrived. Valverde cried out to Pizarro and his men, calling on them to strike the Incas who had first refused and then insulted the word of God. In the name of the Lord he forgave them for the killing that they would commit, and Pizarro gave the order to fire. Trumpets were sounded and the first shot was fired from the cannon, strategically placed on the usnu platform in the centre of the town. Then the Spaniards – dressed in full armour – charged into the unarmed Incas, who, in their panic at this unexpected attack, crushed one another as they attempted to escape. Pizarro and his men approached Atahualpa and, after killing the Lord of Chincha, hacked to death one after the other of his royal litter-bearers, then overturned the litter and seized the god-emperor.

The Spaniards continued slaughtering the Incas who were unable to defend themselves. More and more were killed, some being crushed to death and others put to the sword. Then a wall of the town collapsed under the press of bodies and some Incas were able to escape. The Spaniards raced their horses across the plain, cutting down as many of the fleeing soldiers as they could.

The attack had several unexpected benefits for Pizarro. He had captured the enemy leader in his first military action. In addition, Atahualpa was an absolute ruler whose orders would be obeyed even though he was held captive. Third, the Inca Emperor had surrounded himself with a bodyguard not of soldiers but of his most important counselors and officials – the administrators of the empire. Now that all were dead, the quick and ruthless action of the Spaniards had won the day against almost impossible odds. Atahualpa had misjudged the newcomers and now the most powerful ruler in the Americas had been captured by a handful of brave but reckless adventurers.

The *Sapa* Inca was quick to observe that his new masters were greedy for anything made of gold and silver. He offered to fill the room he was standing in once with gold, then twice over with silver – and all within two months. Pizarro accepted this astonishing offer and the imperial order went out to all parts of the empire. Soon, llama caravans were making their way across the Andes to Cajamarca laden down with the ransom – priceless works of art belonging to the Incas and possibly also older pieces belonging to their predecessors. As each load arrived the beautiful objects were broken up so that more could be squeezed into the chamber. Possibly for this reason it took six months rather than two to fill the room. At Atahualpa's suggestion, Pizarro sent three of his men to Cuzco to supervise the ransom's collection at the capital. When the Incas there refused to pillage the golden images of the Sun god from the Coricancha they were horrified to see the Spaniards help themselves.

At Easter of the following year reinforcements of 150 men under Pizarro's former partner, Diego de Almagro, arrived in Cajamarca. It was then that Atahualpa became sure that Pizarro's promise to set him free when the ransom had been paid was a lie. It was clear that the Spanish were in Peru to stay and that his empire would be carved up between them. The great artworks gathered from all over Tawantinsuyu began to be melted down in May of that year – some 11 tons of gold and 26,000 pounds of silver. Pizarro sent his brother Hernando Pizarro back to Spain with the royal fifth for the king, along with a sample of some intact pieces including a silver eagle and a golden statue.

Once the collected masterpieces had been turned into ingots, stamped and weighed, they were distributed to every Spanish soldier. Each cavalryman received 90 pounds of gold and 180 pounds of silver, while a foot soldier received half this amount. Pizarro's officers and the royal officials who were present received more, and Pizarro himself the most – more than double a cavalryman's share.

Once they had received their booty the Spaniards had something to lose and they became increasingly nervous. They argued about Atahualpa's fate and decided that it would be too dangerous to honour their word and set him free. Rumours of advancing Inca armies and Atahualpa's ordering of the death of the captive Huascar, combined with the lust of

Almagro's men for new conquests and treasures of their own, proved fatal for the *Sapa* Inca. Pizarro was convinced that Atahualpa should be executed. In this decision he received the support and blessing of his men and despite the Inca Emperor's strenuous arguments in his own defence his fate was sealed.

On the evening of Saturday 26 July 1533, Atahualpa was put to death. He should have been burnt at the stake, but was given the opportunity of a more civilized end by garotting if he converted to Christianity. For the Incas, it was important that the body remained intact after death so that it could be mummified and added to the line of past emperors in order to become a deified ancestor. Probably for this reason Atahualpa allowed himself to be baptized, but Spanish hypocrisy knew no bounds. After being strangled the emperor's body had fire thrown upon it, the remains being given a Christian burial, while Pizarro wept. Within a few days his body had been spirited away, mummified and hidden somewhere in the surrounding mountains.

This had been one of the most astonishing events in the history of the world. A handful of tough and greedy adventurers had gambled everything and won, overturning the mightiest empire the Americas had ever seen. Now they could turn their attention to ransacking the remaining wealth of Tawantinsuyu.

With Atahualpa's death the empire lay open. Pizarro moved quickly, taking advantage of the splits between Huascar's faction in Cuzco and Atahualpa's supporters. A member of Huascar's royal line, Tupac Huallpa, became Pizarro's puppet ruler and at his coronation at Cajamarca all the assembled chiefs and officials took an oath of allegiance to the Spanish crown. Accompanied by the new emperor, the Inca General Chalcuchima, and many of Huascar's officials, Pizarro finally left Cajamarca and marched south towards Cuzco.

As this strange band of Spaniards and Incas made their way along the Inca royal roads they found much support. Those who had championed Huascar in the civil war and others who had been only recently conquered welcomed him. In their enthusiasm they saw only the opportunities which Atahualpa's death offered them rather than the true nature of the white invaders. The remnants of

Atahualpa's army occasionally gave battle, but the combined effect of the Spaniards' horses, armour and razor-sharp swords of Toledo steel proved too much for the lightly armed Inca troops. There was also the psychological effect of horses, which the Incas had never seen before. These strange animals accompanied the invaders, who themselves may have been seen as supernatural beings or gods in the superstitious world of Inca mythology. As we have seen already, the Spaniards were called *viracochas* by Andean peoples long after the conquest.

On the way to Cuzco Pizarro stopped briefly at the city of Jauja to rest his men. During this time Tupac Huallpa died in mysterious circumstances, possibly poisoned by Atahualpa's supporters. Pizarro split his small army, sending Hernando de Soto and his cavalry ahead to secure the strategic bridges and obtain food from the imperial storehouses. De Soto had several skirmishes with Inca troops, but finally made it to the great Apurímac river. The huge suspension bridge which spanned the river had been destroyed by Atahualpa's forces, but fortunately for the Spanish the river level was low and they were able to cross. As they struggled exhausted onto the far bank, the Incas attacked, killing five Spaniards and wounding many. Again fortune smiled on De Soto, as a group of conquistadors sent by Pizarro arrived during the night and, between them, the two Spanish forces pushed their way through the Inca ranks.

De Soto and Pizarro now linked up again for the advance to Cuzco, and were unexpectedly joined by an Inca prince called Manco. Pizarro appointed Manco his new puppet-ruler and the grateful Inca immediately betrayed Chalcuchima, accusing him of instigating the recent attacks on the Spaniards and poisoning the hapless Tupac Huallpa. Pizarro acted immediately, and had the old general burnt to death. After one last fruitless battle with the Spanish the remainder of Atahualpa's men, under the General Quisquis, retreated north to Quito, and Pizarro and his conquistadors finally entered Cuzco. Soon after, amid the elaborate ceremonial accorded to new emperors, Manco officially became the *Sapa* Inca and was given the red tassles of office.

Both sides remained wary of each other, but the Spaniards were at last able to indulge their appetite for treasure. They sacked the imperial city, stripping the gold sheeting from the temples and plundering the tombs of their accumulated wealth. It wasn't long before they turned their attention to the Coricancha and, ignoring the protests of the high priest, set about pillaging the many gold and silver animal figures and statues stored inside the Sun god's temple. When all these treasures were melted down, there were several tons of gold and over 50 tons of silver.

Even this vast wealth did not satisfy Pizarro and his men for long. Dazzled by the incredible riches they had won so easily, they were now possessed by gold fever. They set about ravaging the country, torturing and burning alive those who they thought might be able to reveal the whereabouts of more hidden treasures. More often than not these treasures were imaginary, but the horrors committed were not. Along with the Spaniard's passion for gold and silver went an unbridled lust for Inca women. Neither the *acllas* in the convents nor the women of noble birth were safe from abuse. Pizarro himself, though hardly a young man, set the precedent by taking a teenaged

Inca princess and having an illegitimate daughter by her.

The cruelty of the Spaniards seemed to know no bounds. They brought with them to South America a system of abuse which they had perfected elsewhere in the Americas, notably the Caribbean and Mexico. This was the *encomienda*, where a Spaniard was awarded the rights to the labour of a group of native peoples. Animals, food, water, clothing, wood and metal were extorted from the indigenous people as well as their services as farmers, servants and porters. All the labour and produce, which had once filled the elaborate network of Inca storehouses and kept an empire well fed, now enriched only those Spaniards who held *encomienda* rights over the local people.

After several years as Pizarro's puppet, Manco at last saw the true nature of his masters. He was increasingly insulted by their behaviour towards him, their constant demands for imaginary treasure, and the reports of his high priest Villac Umu who had witnessed their brutal behaviour on an expedition to Chile. He fled his capital, but was quickly recaptured and had to endure renewed Spaniard demands for gold while suffering the indignity of being shackled with chains. In 1536 Pizarro's brother Hernando set Manco free after he had promised to bring more gold. Instead, Manco escaped to the mountains, where he joined a gathering army which had been raised in secret. The vanguard of this new Inca army encamped around Cuzco, which at this time was occupied by less than 200 Spaniards. In May of that year they attacked, bitterly fighting their way through the city's narrow streets, and then setting fire to the thatched roofs with burning slingstones. In only a few days the city had been burnt and the Incas were in almost total control.

Once again the Spaniards gambled on a reckless move. After spending a night in prayer, some fifty horsemen broke out of the city and, with the help of their Amerindian allies, recaptured the heights in front of the great temple-fortress of Sacsayhuaman overlooking Cuzco. For days there was fierce hand-to-hand fighting. Attacks, repulses and counter-attacks continued until, finally, the Spaniards used scaling-ladders to capture the fortress, and then massacred the remaining Inca soldiers. This was a critical moment. While Cuzco was besieged for another ten months, and rescue missions sent by Francisco Pizarro from the coast were wiped out, the Inca army could not break back into the city. Eventually the Inca soldiers began drifting back to the land to harvest their crops. Pizarro's compatriot, Almagro, finally lifted the siege in April 1537 after returning from Chile.

Manco remained defiant at the town of Ollantaytambo north of Cuzco, but was soon convinced it was necessary to abandon the ancestral Inca homeland and retreat instead to the distant forested region of Vilcabamba and set up his headquarters at Vitcos. Almagro sent Rodrigo Orgóñez in hot pursuit but, although Vitcos was taken by surprise and some members of the *Sapa* Inca's family captured, Manco himself escaped. He quickly realized the need for an even more remote hiding place, and his followers built the city of Vilcabamba, a further two days march from Vitcos, deep within inaccessible forests. The next move saw Francisco Pizarro's brother Gonzalo lead an assault on Vilcabamba, but when he entered the stronghold he discovered that Manco once again had slipped away ever deeper into the jungle. Francisco Pizarro was furious and vented his anger by torturing and burning alive those Incas who had surrendered at Vitcos and then raping and murdering Manco's sister.

For the next six years, the small Inca kingdom at Vilcabamba was left in peace as the Spanish conquistadors argued among themselves. One consequence of this was that both Almagro and Francisco Pizarro were killed and that control of Peru was regained for the Spanish crown by the victory of a royal army over the remnants of Almagro's supporters. Yet even these internal squabbles spelled disaster for the Incas when Manco was murdered by five of Alamagro's men to whom he had given sanctuary at Vilcabamba.

In the years that followed resentment against the Spaniards grew among the indigenous people of the Andes. Eventually, after many efforts by the Spanish to lure the Incas from Vilcabamba, they succeeded in persuading one of Manco's sons to emerge. In typical Inca fashion, however, another son ruled in his place and the Spaniards gained nothing. This son, Titu Cusi Yupanqui, died of natural causes in 1571 and was succeeded by his brother, Tupac Amaru. Meanwhile a new Spanish viceroy had arrived in Peru. Francisco de Toledo soon decided to destroy Vilcabamba once and for all. In June 1572 his forces marched north and finally broke into the city. They found the temples and palaces abandoned and the buildings still smoking from having been set on fire by the Incas before their departure.

Toledo's men were determined not to repeat past mistakes by letting the Inca ruler escape. They cut their way through dense jungle paths in pursuit on hearing that Tupac Amaru had taken refuge with jungle Amerindians. Travelling by night through the lush undergrowth the Spanish crept up on the ruler who was sitting with his wife around a camp fire. The expedition returned to Cuzco in triumph in September, dragging Tupac Amaru behind them in chains, along with a golden statue of Inti and the sacred mummies of Manco Inca and Titu Cusi Yupanqui.

Tupac, like Atahualpa before him, eventually converted to Christianity but was nevertheless tried and sentenced to death. On the day of his execution, the air was full of the sound of grieving Incas gathered in Cuzco and on the surrounding hills. Even some Spaniards wept openly for the last emperor. After receiving absolution and renouncing the Inca gods, Tupac Amaru was decapitated and all the bells in Cuzco's churches and monasteries began to toll. So ended the final tragic act in the cataclysm which engulfed the successors of Pachacuti and Tupac Yupanqui.

Aftermath

The Inca Empire was built on the accumulated achievements of three thousand years, but lasted less than a century. Deeply rooted in native social and religious traditions, Pachacuti and Tupac Yupanqui nevertheless created something new. These two men had a clear vision of empire and the skills and energy to make it work. Yet it would be a mistake to see the Inca imperial design, in hindsight, as a somehow natural development or an unqualified success. Beyond Cuzco, Inca culture was imposed and maintained by force. The resentment this caused among local people, who were not ethnically Inca, is apparent in the many rebellions which had to be suppressed. Here also lies part of the answer to the often asked question, 'How could a handful of Spanish conquistadors destroy an empire of millions?'

The reply is, they did not. Pizarro's men were welcomed by disaffected Incas and those who sought to regain their independence by throwing off Inca control. The Spaniards were fed, watered, guided, advised and reinforced by large numbers of native Andean peoples during the conquest. If they had not been, the outcome might well have been very different. Only too late did these various factions and tribal groups realize that they had traded one master for another infinitely more cruel and demanding. The savagery and injustices of the conquest, and the terrible legacies of abuse, poverty and disease during the colonial period, etched themselves deeply into the indigenous Andean mind and echoed down the centuries to the present day. Yet somehow the dignity and traditions of native Andean peoples have survived.

Today's visitor to Peru is overwhelmed by the splendours of Inca civilization built in a harsh and literally breathtaking landscape. It is the uniqueness of the Inca achievement, rather than the depredations of the conquest, which leaves a lasting impression. And the people are still there. Young Quechua-speaking children dressed in multi-coloured traditional costumes run between the monumental carved stones at Ollantaytambo, pose for photographs in the Inca streets of Cuzco, and watch their mothers weave with the traditional back-strap loom used by their ancestors. In countless street markets maize, coca, potatoes, and fertility charms are still sold, alongside a dazzling variety of souvenirs.

It is perhaps the ultimate irony that, after five hundred years, the lives of some indigenous Andean peoples are only now beginning to improve, with money from tourists drawn to the architectural wonders created by their own Inca ancestors. The present is indeed a product of the past. It may be that the real treasure of the Incas was never gold and silver, but the enduring spirit of the people themselves.

Glossary

aclla	a 'chosen woman'
aclla huasi	house of the 'chosen women'
ayllu	lineage group or kin-based community
cacique	Spanish term for *curaca*
camayoc	an official or craftsman
capac hucha	human sacrificial victim
ceque	sacred lines of spiritual power radiating out of the Coricancha (Temple of the Sun) in Cuzco
chasqui	official Inca messenger
Coya	Inca queen or high-ranking woman
curaca	Amerindian chief, principal chief of a village
El Niño	the climatic event producing torrential rains and flooding
Mama cuna	literally 'mothers', women who had taken a vow of chastity and dedicated themselves to the Inca religion, sometimes called the 'Virgins of the Sun'
mita	system of labour tax
mitmaq	people sent by the Incas to colonize newly conquered areas and aid integration into the empire
moiety	Symbolic half or division into which Inca society was divided

95

Ñusta	the emperor's daughter or a young woman of noble Inca birth
Pachacamac	pre-Inca oracle site and pilgrimage centre on Peru's central coast, later integrated into the Inca Empire
panaqa	royal *ayllu* of male descendants
quipu	system of knotted strings used to record information and possibly historical events and songs
sinchi	war chief
Suyu	a region or division, a quarter, as in Tawantinsuyu
tambo	a way-station/storehouse or inn sited along an Inca highway
Tawantinsuyu	literally 'the land of the four quarters', the Inca name for their empire
usnu	stone throne used by the emperor on ceremonial occasions

Further Reading

Ascher, M. and Ascher, R. *The Code of the quipu: A Study in Media, Mathematics, and Culture* (Ann Arbor, University of Michigan Press, 1981)

Bauer, B.S., *The Development of the Inca State* (Austin, University of Texas Press, 1992)

Bauer, B.S. and Dearborn, D.S.P. *Astronomy and Empire in the Ancient Andes* (Austin, University of Texas Press, 1995)

Berrin, K. (ed.), *The Spirit of Ancient Peru* (London, Thames & Hudson, 1997)

Betanzos, J. de, *Suma y narración de los Incas.* (Madrid, V Centenario del Descubrimiento de América, 1987 [1551])

Bingham, H., *Machu Picchu: A Citadel of the Incas* (New York, Hacker Art Books, 1970)

Bruhns, K.O., *Ancient South America* (Cambridge University Press, 1994)

Brundage, B.C., *Lords of Cuzco* (Norman, University of Oklahoma Press, 1985)

Cieza de León, P. de, *The Incas of Pedro de Cieza de León* (Norman, University of Oklahoma Press, 1959 [1553])

Classen, C., *Inca Cosmology and the Human Body* (Salt Lake City, University of Utah Press, 1993)

Cobo, B., *History of the Inca Empire* (Austin, University of Texas

Press, 1983 [1653])

——, *Inca Religion and Customs* (Austin,University of Texas Press, 1990 [1653])

Conrad, G.W. and Demarest, A.A. *Religion and Empire: The dynamics of Aztec and Inca expansionism* (Cambridge University Press, 1984)

D'Altroy, T.N., *Provincial Power in the Inca Empire* (Washington DC, Smithsonian Institution Press, 1993)

Demarest, A.A., *Viracocha – The Nature and Antiquity of the Andean High God* (Cambridge, Mass., Peabody Museum, 1981)

Denevan, W., Mathewson, K. and Knapp, G. (eds), *Prehistoric Agricultural Fields in the Central Andes* (Oxford, British Archaeological Reports, 1987)

Dillehay, T.D., 'Tawantinsuyu Integration of the Chillon Valley Peru: A Case of Inca Geo-Political Mastery', *Journal of Field Archaeology* 4 (1977), 397–405

Falk Moore, S., *Power and Property in Inca Peru* (New York, Columbia University Press, 1958)

Farrington, I.S., 'The Mummy, Palace and Estate of Inca Huayna Capac at Quispeguanca', *Tawantinsuyu* 1 (1995), 55–64

Garcilaso de la Vega, R*oyal Commentaries of the Incas and General History of Peru* (Austin, University of Texas Press, 1987 [1609])

Gasparini, G. and Margolies, L., *Inca Architecture*, (Bloomington, Indiana University Press, 1980)

Guaman Poma de Ayala, F., *El primer crónica y buen gobierno*, 3 vols, J.V. Murra and R. Adorno (eds), (Mexico City, Siglo Veintiuno, 1980)

Hemming, J., *Machu Picchu* (London, Newsweek Books, 1981)

——, *The Conquest of the Incas* (Harmondsworth, Penguin, 1983)

——, and Ranney, E. *Monuments of the Incas*, (Albuquerque, University of New Mexico Press, 1990)

Hyslop, J., *The Inca Road System* (New York, Academic Press, 1984)

——, *Inca Settlement Planning*, (Austin, University of Texas Press, 1990)

Jones, J., *Art of Empire: the Inca of Peru* (Greenwich, The Museum of Primitive Art/New york Graphic Society, 1964)

Kendall, A., *Everyday Life of the Incas*, (London, Batsford, 1973)

——, 'Inca planning north of Cuzco between Anta and Machu Picchu and along the Urubamba valley', N.J. Saunders and O. de Montmollin (eds), *Recent Studies in Pre-Columbian Archaeology*, (Oxford, British Archaeological Reports, 1988), pp. 457–88,

Lechtman, H., 'Technologies of Power: The Andean Case', in J.S. Henderson and P.J. Netherly (eds), *Configurations of Power*, (Ithaca, Cornell University Press, 1993), pp. 244-80

MacCormack, S., 'Demons, Imagination, and the Incas', in S. Greenblatt (ed.), *New World Encounters* (Berkeley, University of California Press, 1993), pp. 101–26

McEwan, C. and M. van de Guchte, 'Ancestral Time and Sacred Space in Inca State Ritual', in R.F. Townsend (ed.), *The Ancient Americas: Art from Sacred Landscapes* (Art Institute of Chicago, 1992), pp. 359-71

Morris, C. and Thompson, D.E., *Huánuco Pampa: An Inca City and its Hinterland* (London, Thames & Hudson, 1985)

Morrison, T., *Qosqo: The Navel of the World*, (Chicago, Academy Chicago Publishers, 1992)

Moseley, M.E., *The Incas and their Ancestors* (London, Thames & Hudson, 1992)

Murra, J.V., *The Economic Organization of the Inca State* (Greenwich, JAI Press, 1980)

Niles, S., *Callacha: Style and Status in an Inca Community* (Iowa City, University of Iowa Press, 1987)

——, 'Inca architecture and the Sacred Landscape', in R.F. Townsend (ed.), *The Ancient Americas: Art from Sacred Landscapes* (Art Institute of Chicago, 1991), pp 347–58

——, 'Artist and Empire in Inca and Colonial Textiles', in R. Stone-Miller (ed.), *To Weave for the Sun: Ancient Andean Textiles* (London, Thames & Hudson, 1994)

Patterson, T.C., *The Inca Empire: The Formation and Disintegration of a Pre-Capitalist State* (Oxford, Berg, 1991)

Polo de Ondegardo, J., *Relación de los fundamentos acerca del notable daño que resulta de no guardar a los indios sus fueros* (Lima, Colección libros y documentos referentes a la historia del Peru, Urteaga, 1917 [1571])

Protzen, J.-P., *Inca Architecture and Construction at Ollantaytambo*, (Oxford University Press, 1993)

Reinhard, J., *Machu Picchu, The Sacred Center* (Lima, Nuevas Imágenes, 1991)

——, 'Sacred Peaks of the Andes', *National Geographic* 181: 3 (1992), 84–111

——, 'Peru's Ice Maidens', *National Geographic* 189: 6 (1996) 62–81

Rostworowski de Diez Canseco, M., *History of the Inca Realm* (Cambridge University Press, 1999)

Rowe, J.H., 'Inca culture at the time of the Spanish conquest', in J.H. Steward (ed.), *Handbook of South American Indians* (7 vols), vol. 2, (Washington DC, Smithdown Institution Press, 1946), pp.186–330

——, 'What kind of a Settlement was Inca Cuzco?' *Ñawpa Pacha*, 5 (1967) 59–76

Schaedel, R.P., 'Early State of the Incas', in H. Claessen and P. Skalnik (eds), *The Early State* (The Hague, Mouton, 1978), pp. 289–330

Silverblatt, I., *Moon, Sun, and Witches: Gender Ideologies and Class in Inca and Colonial Peru* (Princeton University Press, 1987)

Spalding, K., *Huarochiri: An Andean Society under Inca and Spanish Rule* (Stanford University Press, 1984)

Urton, G., *At the crossroads of the earth and sky: An Andean cosmology* (Austin, University of Texas Press, 1981)

——, *The History of a Myth: Pacariqtambo and the Origin of the Incas* (Austin, University of Texas Press, 1990)

Von Hagen, A. and Morris, C., *The Cities of the Ancient Andes* (London, Thames & Hudson, 1998)

Wachtel, N., *The Vision of the Vanquished* (New York, Harper & Row, 1977)

Wise, T. and McBride, A., *The Conquistadores.* (Oxford, Osprey Publishing, 1999)

Zuidema, R.T., *The Ceque System of Cuzco* (Leiden, Brill, 1964)

FURTHER READING

GENERAL

There are many good up-to-date books on the civilizations of Pre-Columbian South America which include chapters on the Incas. The beautifully illustrated book by Berrin (1997) reveals the visual splendours of ancient Andean cultures, and for more detailed general accounts Bruhns (1994) and Moseley (1992) are recommended. The classic description of Inca society is still John Rowe's (1946) 'Inca culture at the time of the Spanish conquest', in the *Handbook of South American Indians*. Although old-fashioned in language and approach, it nevertheless provides a magisterial appraisal of every aspect of Inca culture. Kendall (1973, and many reprints) is also somewhat outdated but remains the most accessible popular account. The recent English publication by Rostworowski de Diez Canseco (1999) is an excellent historical analysis by Peru's foremost ethnohistorian, and Conrad and Demarest (1984) compare the Inca and Aztec civilizations in a provocative fashion.

A good place to look for more detailed works is *The Incas: A Bibliography of Books and Periodical Articles*, Hipolito Unanue Bibliographic Series 1, vol. 8 (Washington, DC, 1987). Websites are also increasingly plentiful and useful. The British Library (London, UK) and the Library of Congress (Washington, DC, USA) provide almost instant access to a vast number of books on the subject. The interactive world map on the 'Archnet' website is also a good starting point.

EARLY ACCOUNTS

Unlike Mexico, there is no wealth of pictorial manuscripts for

102

Inca life or the Spanish conquest. The nearest is Guaman Poma de Ayala (1980) which offers many line drawings of people, places, and religious and social life alongside full descriptions. Other valuable accounts of conquest and post-conquest sources, each with its own strengths and weaknesses are Betanzos (1987), Cieza de León (1959), Cobo (1983 and 1990) and Garcilaso de la Vega (1987). Spalding (1984) and Niles (1987) provide valuable anthropological accounts of traditional Andean communities from Inca to modern times, and Classen (1993) offers a unique insight into Inca thought and beliefs.

ARCHAEOLOGY OF INCA CIVILIZATION

Inca archaeology has seen great advances in recent years, particularly concerning architecture, religion, and the relationship between Cuzco and outlying regions. Gasparini and Margolies (1980) and Hemming and Ranney (1990) both offer authoritative texts with stunning photographs that capture the skill of Inca architects and stonemasons. Hyslop (1984) offers a unique study of the Inca road system, and Morris and Thompson (1985) throw light on the nature of the Inca Empire beyond the capital at Cuzco. The most dramatic aspect of Inca archaeology in recent years has been the discoveries of high-altitude mummies of Inca human sacrifices, and Reinhard (1992 and 1996) captures the excitement in well-written and beautifully illustrated popular articles. Hemming (1983, and many reprints) is the best account of the Spanish conquest, and Wachtel (1977) explains the same tragic events from the Inca perspective.

Index